Eli W. Caruthers

A Brief History of Col. David Fanning

Also, Naomi Wise, or the wrongs of a beautiful girl: and Randolph's manufacturing

Eli W. Caruthers

A Brief History of Col. David Fanning
Also, Naomi Wise, or the wrongs of a beautiful girl: and Randolph's manufacturing

ISBN/EAN: 9783337419424

Printed in Europe, USA, Canada, Australia, Japan

Cover: Foto ©ninafisch / pixelio.de

More available books at **www.hansebooks.com**

A BRIEF HISTORY

OF

COL. DAVID FANNING,

ALSO

Naomi Wise, or the wrongs of a beautiful Girl,

AND

RANDOLPH'S MANUFACTURING.

Price 50 Cents.

HARRELL'S PRINT, WELDON, N. C.

WHIG AND TORY OFFICERS—COLONEL DAVID FANNING HIS EARLY LIFE.

REVOLUTIONARY times not only " try men's souls, " but test their principles and develope their character When society is resolved into its original elements and there is no master spirit to control the perturbed and excited mass; when, for the present, all law and government are virtually set aside, except, perhaps, martial law, which can neither take cognizance of all the cases of wrong that occur, nor reach the whole of a large community scattered over a widely extended territory; and when every one, feeling that " where there is law there can be no transgression," does as he pleases and gives full scope to his good or bad passions, as the one or the other may happen to be prevalent, a man may become as much distinguished by his vices as by his virtues,—by a course of rapine, murder, and atrocious villanies, as by the wisdom of his counsels wherever they may be needed, or by his deeds of valor on the field of battle. In the war of the Revolution in this country, which resulted in the unprecedented freedom and prosperity which we enjoy, the patriots of that day, who toiled and suffered and shed their blood in the cause of independence, in-scribed their names indelibly on the rolls of fame: and, while the world stands, will command the veneration and gratitude of mankind; but there were others who were then about as conspicuous, and who, by an opposite course, have rendered their names quite as immortal.

Of this latter class, some of whom were to be found in every State of the confederacy, Col. David Fanning stood pre-eminent in North Carolina; but when we consider his origin and his early life, we cannot be so much surprised at his after course. With a native intellect which, under proper culture, would have made him prominent anywhere or in any cause, his powers were developed under the influence of poverty, disease and neglect, without early instruction or example, and without any moral or religious training. Regarded, it seems, wherever known, as an outcast from genteel society, he never received any favors, or had any kind attentions paid him except from pity on account of his forlorn condition. Under these circumstances, those strong feelings which usually accompany a vigorous intellect, instead of being softened and directed into the proper channel by the hallowing influences of religion, or even by the courtesies and bland influences of intelligent and refined society, were embittered and strengthened for evil by the ungracious treatment which he received, and afterwards, by impelling him to the commission of crimes which spread sorrow and distress over the country, gave him a most unenviable notoriety, and made his name, not only from that time to the present, but for generations to come, a reproach and a by-word of infamy

In the University Magazine, for March, 1853, there is an interesting communication from Governor Swain, in which he gives the following summary account of Fanning's birth-place, his early life, and his entrance on his military career. David Fanning was born of obscure parents, in the county of Wake, about the year 1754, and apprenticed to a loom maker. He removed to Chatham in 1778 and followed his trade until the occupation of Wilmington, by Major Craig, presented other prospects to his imagination. Very shortly thereafter, clad in a long white hunting shirt, and mounted on a common draft horse, he was found at the head of a band of marauders, not more than 8 or 10 in number. His head-quarters were, to some extent, at the house of John Reins on Brush creek; but he had no horse, seldom lodged in a house, generally passed his nights in solitary and unfrequented places, sometimes with companions, but more frequently alone. He and his colleagues were spoken of as "out liers". His first marauding expedition is said to have been to Deep river; and the earliest sufferers from his rapacity and violence, were Charles Shearing, 'and Captains Duck and Dye. He went to Shearings' in the night, shot him as he ran from the house, took his gun, scoured the neighborhood and returned to Reins'. His energy, capacity, and courage were duly appreciated by Major Craig, who appointed him Colonel of the loyal mliitia of Randolph and Chatham, clothed him in British uniform and presented him a sword and holster of pistols. An old royalist, named Lindly, gave him a mare called the "Red Doe," from her peculiar color. This animal, whose blood is still traced and highly estimated at the present day, became subsequently almost as famous as her master. One of the most interesting episods in Fanning's history relates to the circumstances under which he lost her."

We have given the above extract entire, partly because the well known accuracy of the writer in every thing that relates to North Carolina history, entitles it to high consideration, and partly because it brings before us in a small space the leading events of Fanning's early life. It differs considerably, however, in some particulars, from the accounts which I had previously obtained from other sources; but on a subject, for the knowledge of which we have all to rely, for the most part, on traditionary statements, some discrepancies, at least in circumstances of minor importance, are to be expected; and we shall just state such facts, in the course of the narrative, as rest on the authority of those whose opportunities for ascertaining the truth were good, and who had made it their business to investigate the subject.

Several of the following pages are taken, in substance, from the papers of Mr. McBride; but as those papers consisted chiefly of very short notes, something like a lawyer's "brief," I have not used the quotation marks. As he collected his materials some twenty-five years ago, more or less, he must have had, at that time, great facilities for ascertaining the truth; and from his habits of legal investigation we might expect that his inquiries on this subject would be conducted with something of the same precision. It is to be regretted that so many of his papers were lost; but I imagine that most of what related to the birth-place of Fanning and to his history until he became a British officer, has been preserved; and although no one could write off these notes as he would have done himself, since he could have supplied much from memory and from further inquiries as he progressed, yet we feel gratified that we have so many of the main facts. He tells us that he got his information from James Johnson, a man whom he considered as good authority; and therefore it would seem that his statements ought to be regarded as altogether reliable. Johnson was the nephew of John O'Deniell, with whom Fanning, when a mere youth, lived for two or three years; and of course, he had a good opportunity of becoming acquainted with his history. He told McBride that although he was only eight or nine years old when Fanning came into his uncle's family, he had a distinct recollection of him,--his appearance, condition and deportment; that he was at his uncle's house most of the time that Fanning was there; and that he had often heard the facts related afterwards by his uncle, who was still living at the time when he gave Mr. McBride this information.

Without assuming any further responsibility than to give the facts thus obtained, and to inform the reader of the source whence they were derived, we proceed with the narrative. According to these papers, David Fanning was born in Johnson County, then a part of Wake, in the year 1756 or 1757, and of low parentage. When a boy, he was bound to a Mr. Bryant, of that County, from whom he ran away when he was about 16 or 17 years of age; and after wandering over the country for some time on foot, he came to the house of John O'Deniell, who lived in Orange County, a little below the Hawfield settlement. Fanning stated to Mr. O'Deniell, as his reason for leaving his master, that he had treated him with great severity and neglect, making him live in the woods to take care of his cattle, and without comfortable food or clothing. O'Deniell took him in, merely from feelings of compassion; for he was a miserable object, being almost naked, and what clothes he had on were ragged and dirty.

He had also the scald head, or tetter worm, which had been neglected, until it had taken the hair all off his head, except perhaps a very little low down about the neck, which had to be cut off; and the smell was so offensive that he never eat at the table with the family and never slept in a bed. In fact, he seemed to be so conscious of this himself that he was unwilling, even if he had been permitted, either to eat or sleep with other people until he could get better clothing and be cured of his disease. By the kind attentions of Mrs. O'Deniell and the family, he was cured of the tetter, but having lost his hair, he always wore a silk cap on his head under his hat; and, it is said, that his most intimate friends never saw his head bare. While here, he learned to read and write a little, and this opened to him sources of information and furnished him with a medium of communication without which he never could have pursued a course so reproachful to himself and so calamitous to the country. He seemed to be very grateful to O'Deniell and the family for the kindness which they had shown him. He conducted himself, while there, with as much propriety as could be expected; and he often spoke of them in after life with great respect. While living there, he may have worked at his trade of building houses or making looms, as Governor Swain has stated; but he is said to have been famous for his skill and dexterity in breaking or taming wild horses, which nobody else could manage. Stout of his age, and being afraid of nothing, he could, in a little time, subdue the most fractious and unmanageable horse that came in his way.

In the course of two or three years, when he was about nineteen, more or less, he went into South Carolina, and got in with William O'Deniell, a brother, I presume, or near relative of his former benefactor, who lived on the Pedee, in South Carolina, and near the north line. There he commenced Indian trader, and was carrying on a gainful traffic with the Catawba Indians, by exchanging guns, calicoes, beads and such articles as suited their fancy, for their furs and deerskins, which he carried on pack horses to the sea port towns, and sold them for a very handsome profit; but he had not more than fairly embarked in this gainful buisness, when the difficulties with England commenced. At first he declared himself a Whig: but on his return from one of his trading expeditions, he was met by a little party of lawless fellows, who called themselves Whigs, and robbed him of every thing he had. Without waiting to inquire whether they really belonged to the Whig party or were a mere set of desperadoes, having no settled principles, and with no object but plunder, he at once changed sides; and in the impetuosity and violence of his temper swore vengeance on the whole of the Whig party.

From his subsequent history, it appears that he kept his word, or his oath, with the most rigid fidelity: for, whenever and wherever an opportunity occured, his vindictive spirit was gratified to the full extent of his power; and henceforth we find him engaged, with unremitting ardor in destroying the lives and property of his enemies.

He then joined the Tories on the Pedee; and, it is said, that he was, for some time associated with the famous Colonel McGirth. As they seem to have been kindred spirits, and to have resembled each other very much in some of the most important events of their life, we copy, for the gratification of our readers, the following account of McGirth, from Johnson's Traditions and Reminiscences of the war in the South:—

"Daniel McGirth was a respectable young man, a native of Kirshaw District, nearly related to the Canteys of that neighborhod. He had married a very amiable lady of Sumter District, aunt of the late much respected Matthew James, Esq. McGirth, from his early attachments and associates, joined with his father and relatives cordially in opposition to the claims of the British government. Being a practised hunter and excellent rider, he was well acquainted with the woods and roads and paths in that extensive range of country, extending from Santee river to the Catawba nation on the east of Wateree river. He was highly valuable to the Americans for the facility with which he acquired information of the enemy, and for the accuracy and minuteness with which communicated what he had obtained. He had brought with him into the service a favorite mare, his own property, an elegant animal, on which he felt safe from pursuit, when engaged in the dangerous but important duties of a scout; he called her the Grey Goose. This fine mare was coveted by one of the American officers, at Satilla, in Georgia, who tried various means to obtain possession of her, all of which were opposed by McGirth, chiefly on the ground that she was essentially necessary to the American interest, in the duties performed by him; and without her he could no longer engage in them. The officer continuing urgent, McGirth said or did something to get rid of him, which he might have intended only as a personal rebuff, but probably was much more. He was arrested, tried by a court martial, found guilty of violating the rules and articles of war, and sentenced to the public whipping-post, for a breach of subordination, which could not be overlooked in an army. He suffered the whipping and exposure, and was again committed to prison, waiting to receive another whipping according to his sentence. While thus situated he saw his favorite mare, observed where she was picketed, and immediately began to concert measures for his escape, and the repossession of his mare. He succeeded in both, and, when seated on her back, he turned deliberately round, notwithstanding the alarm at his escape, and denounced vengeance against all the Americans for his ill-treatment. He executed his threats most fully, most fearfully, most vindictively. Indulging this savage, vindictive temper, was indeed productive of great injury to the American cause, and of much public and private suffering, but it was also the cause of his own ruin and misery. When the State was again recovered by the American army, he still kept in the woods, retreated into Georgia, and thence into Florida. When Florida was reconveyed to the Spaniards, by the treaty of peace, he became subject to their laws or suspicions, was arrested, and confined by them five years in one of their damp dungeons in the Castle of St. Augustine, where his health was totally destroyed. When discharged from St. Augustine, he with much difficulty returned to his wife in Sumter District. McGirth's father was a captain in the South Carolina militia at the time of his son's defection, but continued firmly and devotedly attached to the interests of his country."

How long Fanning continued with McGirth, and in what deeds of atrocity he was engaged, we have no means of ascertaining; but from his connection with one who was not only his equal, if no more, in native capacity and energy of character, but greatly his superior in education and in his knowledge of the ways and means of doing harm in such a country and in such a state of things as then existed, we may suppose that he was much better prepared than he would otherwise have been for the course which he subsequently pursued. It was probably the best school for developing and maturing the original elements of his character that he could have found; and, judging from his achievments in this State, not long after, we may infer that he must have made uncommon proficiency. According to McBride's papers and most other accounts which I have had, he is not known to have been in North Carolina from the beginning of the war, or a little before it, until the beginning of the year 1781, when he came into the State along with the British army under Lord Cornwallis, or about the same time; but he did not continue with it; nor did he, for some time, hold any commission or have any men properly under his command.

From his natural temper, and from his early habits, he was a *sui juris* kind of a man, and neither knew nor cared much about the military rules and tactics of modern warfare. He could not be subjected to the strictness of military discipline, nor was he calculated for the slow and measured movements of regular armies. His irascible and vindictive temper could not endure the custom of civilized nations in showing humanity to the conquered, and in giving protection to the feeble. He gloried not in success, because he believed it to be necessary to the welfare of his country, nor in the triumph of valor on the field of honest contest, but in the capture and extermination of his enemies. A stranger to that manly courage which is sustained and guided by great moral principles, he was just fitted for the course which he pursued, the guerilla mode of warfare, in which there have been few in modern times who have surpassed him, either in the rapidity of his movements, or in the number and atrocity of his deeds. With the astuteness of the Indian and the fleetness of the Arab, with a constitution capable of bearing almost any amount of toil; and with a patience of hunger and fatigue worthy of any cause, he might be said to be always on horseback and always in motion. He was often upon his enemies when they were least expecting it; and having accomplished his purpose of death or devastation, he was gone before their friends could rally. Often, when supposed to be at a distance, the alarm of his presence in a neighborhood was communicated by the smoke of burning houses, and by the cries of frightened and flying women and children.

In the communication to the University Magazine, already noticed, Governor Swain says, that " he removed to Chatham in 1778, and followed his trade until the occupation of Wilmington, by Major Craig, presented other prospects to his imagination," but takes no notice of his going into South Carolina, and was probably not aware of the fact. There is however no real contradiction or discrepancy between his statement and the one which I have made on the authority of McBride's papers; for Fanning may have returned to Chatham sooner than was known to McBride or his correspondents, and may have worked at his trade for a short time; but, having been with McGirth in South Carolina, and engaged in the bold and vindictive operations of that adventurous spirit, it is not probable that he would again engage unless from necessity or considerations of policy, in the dull business of building houses or making looms, so uncongenial to his nature, so foreign from his settled purposes, and so much below the ambitious aspirings which had now got the ascendency in his mind.

So far as my enquiries had gone, I could find no intimation of his being in North Carolina, after the beginning of the war, until February 25th, 1781, when he was at Pyle's famous "hacking match," on that memorable day, but held no commission, and of course from the peculiar circumstances of that whole affair he could take no part, unless he had stood in the ranks and submitted like the rest to be hacked into pieces, which was not according to his taste, and he was not to be caught in such a trap. When Col. Lee, at the head of his Legion, was riding along the line of deluded Tories, who had been drawn up for the purpose of receiving Colonel Tarleton, as they supposed, and were shouting "hura for King George," Fanning called out to them repeatedly that those men were the American cavalry, and not the British; but, as General Green with his whole army had run out of the State only a few days before, and as the British army, apparently exulting in its power, was so near, they could not believe that an American corps would dare to show itself almost in sight of Lord Cornwallis, and warnings were in vain. When he saw that his efforts to undeceive them were of no avail, he withdrew to a place of safety where he could see the commencement of the havoc made on his friends; but as soon as he saw that their destruction was inevitable, he prudently fled and took care for his own safety. If, on that day, so fatal to the Tories and so auspicious to the cause of American freedom, the command had devolved on Fanning instead of Colonel Pyle, the result would probably have been very different; but an all-wise Providence ordered otherwise, and we have reason to rejoice in this development of his benignant and unchanging purposes.

A crisis was now approaching in the long and arduous struggle for independence. Throughout the State, all inteligent and reflecting men, on both sides, were expecting and desiring a general battle, which it was believed would either give the British forces a complete ascendency in the South, or turn the tide so much against them that further efforts on their part would be useless. The discomfiture of the Tories, under Colonel Pyle, may be regarded as a fortunate prelude to the battle which was fought a few days after near Martinville, at which we presume Col. Fanning was present. The probability is that, after Pyle's defeat, he either fell in with the British army until after the battle, or "mounted on a common draft horse," and attended by a few followers, daring and reckless spirits like himself, he was ranging through the country plundering provisions for his foreign friends, giving them whatever information he could obtain, and producing terror and distress among the inhabitants. While the British lay in Hillsborough, according to tradition, he committed a number of depredations and cruelties in the Northwest part of the county, but of all that we have no certain information.

Whether he was at the Guilford battle or not is a matter of little consequence. It is known that soon after, and for some time, he had his residence on or near Deep river, and about the mouths of Brush and Richland creeks, where, remaining for a few weeks *in cog*, he took up his lodgings sometimes under the open canopy of heaven, but oftener in the humble dwelling of John Rains, who afterwards became a major in his corps, and one of his most efficient men. Why he never appeared in public nor made himself known, would be useless to enquire. Whether he was only maturing his plans for future operations, or was waiting for a commission from British authority, without which he could not act so efficiently, for which the initiatory steps had, no doubt, been taken, was probably known only to himself, or at most one or two others. If he entered upon his career without a commission he must have had assurance that he might expect one in case he proved his loyalty to the king, and his fitness for command. I had understood, many years ago, that, though he did not receive a formal commission, he got ample encouragement from Lord Cornwallis himself; and, as he had probably given his lordship, some evidence of his valor and of his devotion to the royal cause, either at Clapp's mill or at Martinville; on the strength of this encouragement he commenced operations.

According to the recollections of the old people in that region, at the time when Mr. McBride obtained his information, his first appearance in public was at a church or meeting house, where the people had met on the Sabbath for public worship, and his success was as great, perhaps, as he could have expected. He either did not arrive until about the close of the services, or he had kept out of view; but when the people came out of the house, he was the first object that attracted their attention. Being an entire stranger, and somewhat singular in his appearance, every eye was fixed upon him, and they were all enquiring, one of another, who was that stranger. He had no doubt been well informed, before he came, respecting the character and sentiments of the people there, and knew that he was among friends; for he appeared to be perfectly at his ease. Probably he had been, for sometime, exerting an influence through the agency of his friend Rains, and finding that things were ready for the disclosure of his purposes, he had boldly taken this step. At all events he did not keep them long in suspense, for he soon let them know that his name was Fanning, and that he had been authorized by the king to raise as many men as he could for the purpose of aiding his majesty to suppress the rebellion and to maintain his government. A man of strong intellect and of great apparent confidence in the justness and success of the cause in which he is engaged, hardly ever fails to sway the minds of the multitude: and so it was on the present occasion.

By discanting, with an air of confidence and much earnestness, on the irresistible progress of the British arms, and the immense resources of that nation, the cruelties of the Whig companies which came into that region, and the injustice of the confiscations to which the property of the loyalists has been subjected, the hopelessness of the American cause, and the pitiable condition of the American forces, half naked, half starved and utterly dispirited by defeat, he so worked upon their fears or strengthened their prepossessions that a number joined him on the spot, and this number was gradually increased as he continued his exertions and became more known over the country. All congenial spirits,—men who, like himself, delighted in bold adventure and deeds of cruelty, rallied round his standard without any hesitation, while the idle and dissolute, who were impatient of the restraints imposed by wholesome laws rigidly enforced, and who would rather live by stealth and rapine than in the way of an honorable industry, were easily induced to follow his fortunes.

We shall not undertake to write his biography, nor to give in full tale his deeds of robbery, devastation and wanton barbarity. To do that would require a volume of ampler size, and an abler pen than mine. The time, during which his operations were carried on, was short, only about eighteen months, more or less; but his plans were executed, and his deeds of shame and cruelty were often perpetrated faster than the pen of a ready writer could record them. You might as well undertake to describe, for the same length of time, all the movements of as many flying Scythians, or the atrocities of as many Saracens, when borne along by the swelling tide of religious enthusiasm, and in the full career of triumphant success. We certainly take no pleasure in portraying his character or describing his progress. We would much rather throw his name, with all its painful associations, into the dark stream of Lethe, and let it sink to rise no more; but it seems right that we should make a fair estimate of the price which our liberties cost, as well as of the blessings which they have confered; and to make such an estimate, it is necessary to have something like a full length portrait, not only of the patriots who fought and conquered, but of the men with whose prowess, malignity and cunning they had to contend. If we would cherish a proper regard for the memory of our fathers and mothers of that period, who have bequeathed to us an inheritance so invaluable, we must have before us the sacrifices which they made, the perils which they encountered, and the toils and hardships which they endured. Fanning inflicted more injury on the country, and was more dreaded at the time than any other man, and many of his crimes and deeds of violence would live in the traditions of the people, from age to age, while our institutions endure, though they were never to stain the pages of history.

A few of these, briefly related, may give the reader some idea of the course which he pursued, and may serve as specimens of a long series, continued without interruption to the end of the chapter, and unsoftened by any prominent or important acts of an opposite kind.

HIS FIRST EFFORTS IN THE ROYAL CAUSE.

Some time in the spring of 1781, and near the commencement of his career as the champion of royalty, he had rather an extraordinary affair with one Charles Sherring, a man who was as daring in his courage and as implacable in his temper as himself. The date of this affair is not known; but it was probably before his descent upon

Pittsboro', and yet he must have become an object of some attention, for threats had passed upon both sides, which would hardly have been the case if he had not become known and formidable. He seems to have been remarkable for the correctness of his information respecting every man and every road and locality within the range of his operations, so that he generally knew, before he set out on an expedition, just when to go, what amount of force to take with him, and everything necessary to success; but if, at any time he was misinformed or mistaken in his calculations, he was very fertile in expedients and very prompt to avail himself of any advantage that might be derived from circumstances. The account of this attack on Sherring when written out from the abbreviated notes among McBride's papers, is substantially as follows:

As he made it a point to kill every active and resolute whig that he could get in his power, he had determined to kill Sherring; and for this purpose he went to his house in the night; but having ascertained before hand that he was alone and unguarded, he took no one with him. Sherring either having been apprised of his design, or from the desperate character of the man and the threats, which had been made, being well aware of his danger, was so cautious as not to sleep in the house with his family, but in a little outhouse, which stood a few steps from the dwelling, and had been used for a corn crib. It was made of small pine logs with the bark peeled off, and floored with a kind of hewn slabs called "puncheons."

The night was dark, or at least there was no moon light; but the logs were not close together, and an outsider could look into the inside. As the weather was warm and pleasant, he had lain down in the bottom of the crib, with some thin covering over him and without telling his wife or any body else where he had gone. On searching the house he found that he was not there, and he could get no information as to his whereabouts; but relying on the information given him, he concluded that he must be on the premises and he was intent on finding him out. For this purpose he extinguished the lights and sallied out in the dark, but he could find nothing of him in the stable or any of the places where he thought he might probably be concealed.

It then occurred to him that he might be in the crib; and peeping through the crevices between the logs, dark as the night was, he described something lying on the bottom, which, from the shape, he concluded must be a man, and he fancied he could tell which end was the head. With this impression, after looking steadily for some time to be certain, if he could, he put his rifle between the logs and fired. The ball passed through, between the windpipe and the neck bone of Sherring; but he was not killed. Though so badly wounded and though he had his rifle in his hand, he neither moved nor made the least noise. The pain must have been intense; but he had sense enough and self command enough to lie as still as if he had been a log of wood, and Fanning made no attempt to ascertain the effect of his shot; whether he concluded that he had been mistaken in the object, or that he had accomplished his purpose, and was therefore satisfied, or that the report of the gun might alarm the neighbors and bring them in upon him before he could get away, was never known. He was, however, so cautious and wary, that he did not even look into the crib; but immediately left the premises, without waiting to find out whether he had shot a man or a bag of potatoes.

As soon as he thought Fanning had time to get off the plantation, Sherring, though so badly wounded, thought it neither safe nor prudent to remain there; and setting off forthwith, without waiting to have his wound dressed or even to go into his house, he went eight miles, to Cornelius Tyson's, where he got his wounds dressed and he recovered in a short time. The impression of the people in the neighborhood seems to have been that Fanning really believed he had killed Sherring and that his great caution was the reason of his leaving in such haste. Few nights now passed for several months in which he did not leave his mark somewhere. No whig and no avowed friend to the cause of Independence could feel safe in his house for a single night, if within reach of this scourge of humanity; and no one, however diligent in seeking information and however shrewd at guessing, could possibly tell beforehand, with any sort of probability, when or where he would strike, nor in what direction they might hope to find a refuge.

CAPTURE OF THE COURT IN PITTSBORO'—AND HIS COMMISSION AS COLONEL BY MAJOR CRAIG,

His next move, of which we have any definite information, was one of a much bolder and more important character. Having got some thirty or forty men who acknowledged him as their leader, he dashed into Pittsboro' when the county court was in session, July 15th, 1781, and captured the lawyers, justices, and other officers of the court, with such of the citizens and prominent men in the place as he wanted. Having been thus successful to the full extent of his wishes, he swore the rebels should never hold court there again; and then, without sustaining any loss or meeting with any resistance, he made good his retreat with the whole of his prisoners. Wheeler, in his history of North Carolina, which is a work of considerable interest and importance, says that the court which Fanning broke up, was a court martial; but I had always understood that it was the county court; and I see that it is so stated by Governor Swain, in his communication to the University Magazine. Unfortunately the records of both the county and superior courts of Chatham were destroyed by fire and no authentic information can now be obtained from that source. We have, therefore, nothing to rely upon in relation to this important transaction except tradition; and those traditionary accounts which were first committed to writing, are probably the most reliable. At this time, it appears that Fanning had no horse, or none that was at all fit for the business in which he was engaged; and as his success in attack or his safety in flight would often depend upon the fleetness of the animal which he rode, it was felt to be a matter of vital importance that he should be better mounted. In the University Magazine, Governor Swain says, on the authority, it seems, of Judge Murphy, who did not at all times observe the same precision and accuracy which were necessary in legal investigations, that "an old loyalist, named Lindly, gave him a mare called the "Red Doe," from her peculiar color;" but he was evidently mistaken in the name of the mare and probably in the name also of the donor. The verbal account which I received of this matter, a number of years ago, was, in substance, as follows:

Feeling much elated with the success of his recent enterprise, and having his mind filled with the prospect of still greater achievements, he began immediately to devise ways and means for getting himself better equipped. For this purpose, he went to a gentleman, a friend or acquaintance, by the name of Bell, who was a loyalist, and very independent in his circumstances. After giving him an account of his exploit in Pittsboro, and a sketch of his plans for future operations, he said to him' "Now, Bell, you are a friend to King George, and the best thing you can do for him is to furnish me a horse; for I have none, and am not able to buy. Bell replied that he had none to spare, or none suitable for that purpose; but that there had been, for two or three days, a stray filly on his premises; and he would freely give him all his right and title to her, if she would do him any good.

The filly was without any marks of ownership, or any indications of having been used, and was withal very poor: but she was, for the present, his only chance, and he took her. After putting her in some better order, and giving her a little training, she proved to be the fleetest animal in the whole country. He called her the "Bay Doe,"—bay from her color, and doe from her fleetness; and when on her back, whether he had to attack or flee, he felt perfectly safe. In a short time he got a horse,—whether by rapine or by donation, from his friend Lindly is not known,—which was also very fleet, but not equal to the mare. He called him the "Red Buck;" and in a little time the fame of the "Red Buck" and the "Bay Doe" was nearly co-extensive with that of Fanning himself. Precisely, when or where he got either of these animals, is a matter of little consequence, but with him it was all-important that he should get his prisoners safely delivered to the British authorities at Wilmington. For this purpose he lost no time; but took care to avoid such routes as would probably expose him to an attack of the Whigs. The following account of his progress to and from Wilmington, together with some of his subsequent transactions and several letters, we take from the University Magazine, already referred to, because it is more authentic and satisfactory than any other, and probably contains all the information that can now be got of his doings at that early stage of his progress

Leaving Pittsboro immediately, he went that evening

"to the west side of Deep river, at Beck's, now called Coxe's Ford; and encamped for the night. On the next day, having received a reinforcement of fifteen men, he set out with his prisoners, forty-four in number, for Wilmington. Of the prisoners, three, John Williams. (London, Esquire, attorney at law,) Gen. Ambrose Ramsey, and Col. Griffiths, were permitted to ride, he taking their word of honor not to desert him."

On that evening they reached ten miles and encamped. On the second night, Stephen Lewis and John Short, two of the Tories, deserted. They traveled by ways, and through the woods to McFall's Mill, on the waters of the Raft Swamp, and before passing the swamp, two of the prisoners, Thomas Scurlock and Capt. James Hardin, who Fanning feared would attempt to escape, were handcuffed and so continued to Wilmington. On the other side of the swamp they met Col. McNeill, with one hundred and fifty men, returning from Wilmington. They continued their route on the West side of the river, and encamped opposite to Wilmington.

Gen. Ramsey, John Williams, Esq and Col. Griffiths, who were on their parole of honor, were attended only by one man, Michael Pearson, and rode either before or behind the party as they pleased. At Wilmington they were paroled by Major Craig, and returned. Thomas Scurlock died, and the other prisoners were sent by Major Craig, to Charleston.

The following letter written by the prisoners when on their way to Wilmington, and addressed to Gov. Burke, will be interesting to the reader, and therefore we make no apology for its insertion. We copy from the University Magazine.

GEORGE H. RAMSEY AND OTHERS, TO GOV. BURKE.
Camp at McFall's Mill,
Raft Swamp, July 22d, 1781.

On Tuesday last we were captured at Chatham Courthouse by a party under the command of Col. David Fanning, which party, we found, consisted of persons who complained of the greatest cruelties either to their persons or property. Some had been unlawfully drafted, others had been whipped and illtreated without trial, others had their houses burned and all their property plundered, and barbarous and cruel murders had been committed in their neighborhoods. The officers they complained of, are Major Naul, Capt. Robeson. of Bladen, Capt. Crump, Col. Wade and Phill Alston. The latter, a day or two ago, a few miles in our rear, took a man on the road and put him to death, which has much incensed the Highlanders in this part of the country. A Scotch gentleman, the same day, was taken at one McAffie's mill, and ill-treated. He is said to be a peaceable and inoffensive man. His name we do not know. He lives on the Raft Swamp—should be happy if he could be liberated. Notwithstanding the cruel treatment these people have received, we have been treated with the greatest civility, and with the utmost respect and politeness by our commanding officer, Colonel Fanning, to whom we are under the greatest obligations; and we beg leave to inform your excellency that unless an immediate stop is put to such inhuman practices, we plainly discover the whole country will be deluged in blood and the innocent will suffer for the guilty. We well know your abhorrence of such inhuman conduct and your steady intention to prevent it. All we mean is information. We expect to be delivered to Major Craig, at Wilmington, in two or three days, entirely destitute of money and clothes. How long we shall remain so, God only knows. All we have to ask is, that the perpetrators of such horrid deeds may be brought to trial, that prisoners may be well-treated in the future.

And we are

your Excellency's

Most obedient servants.

This letter was signed by Geo. Herndon Ramsey, Joseph Herndon, Math. Ramsey, W. Kinchen, James Herndon, Thos. Gregory, John Dir Song, James Williams and Thos. Sensbork; and Simon Ferrel was paroled to carry it to the Governor and return to Wilmington. Some of our readers may be a little surprised to find these prisoners speaking so favorably of Col Fanning, and the tories generally in that region; but it is probable that, in this case, they were not allowed to communicate the whole truth nor to make a very frank expression of their feelings. We presume that Fanning would not suffer them to write at all unless he knew the contents of the letter, nor to send it if he found that it contained any statements of which he disapproved.

Under the circumstances, Fanning would have acted unwisely for himself if he had permitted them to say just what they pleased; and being thus restricted; they no doubt thought it was for their interest to compliment him and curry favor with him, so far as they could without compromising their honor or their principles. Fanning, too, must have been pleased with the statements made, for they were just such facts as he wished to have announced to the Governor and if he had not been pleased with it he would not have paroled one of their number solely for the purpose of being the bearer; but there is an expression in a letter which one of them wrote to the Governor after his return, which seems to imply the same thing. James Williams was paroled by Major Craig, in August; and when he returned he addressed to Governor Burke, the following letter, which in the dearth of authentic information, we are glad to get, and which we insert, not only as connected with the preceding; but as throwing some additional light on the state of things at that period.

JAMES WILLIAMS TO GOVERNOR BURKE.

Chatham, 22d. *August*, 1781.

SIR:—I returned yesterday from Wilmington on my parole to Chatham County, which prevents my waiting upon your Excellency in person.

I am desired by the prisoners to acknowledge the receipt of yours by the flag, and to thank you for your promised attention to them. Their case really merits it. Every article to be sold in Wilmington is at least three times as high for hard money as usual. It cost me in three weeks there, for board and some few articles of clothing, £32 sterling, for which I am indebted as they all are, more or less. They desire me to solicit you for a passport for as much tobacco, or any other article, as will discharge the debts. If this should fail, they will be in a very disagreeable situation—their credit will stop and they must inevitably suffer.

I am told your Excellency *understood our letter from McFalls Mill*, Raft Swamp. *We were very unhappy there.*

There has been no news in Wilmington, either by land or water, these six weeks. I brought up two or three of their newspapers, but they are so barren they are not worth enclosing: We hope to be exchanged for shortly.

I am your Excellency's
Most obedient servant,
JAMES WILLIAMS.

To his Excellency Thomas Burke.

After asking the reader to notice the words which we have *made emphatical* for the purpose of calling attention to them, in reference to the preceding letter, we will give the reply of Gov. Burke to the letter which the prisoners wrote to him from McFall's Mill, not because it has any direct bearing upon Fanning, but because it shows the desire of the Executive to maintain the laws and to do justice, as far as possible, to all classes.

GOVERNOR BURKE TO MESSRS. RAMSEY AND OTHERS, PRISONERS TAKEN AT CHATHAM.

State of North Carolina,
July 28th, 1781.

GENTLEMEN:—I have received your letter, dated from McFall's Mill, Raft Swamp, 22d July.

Your having been made prisoners has already been announced to me, but I have not yet obtained sufficient information whereby to determine whether you were acting in a military or civil character at the time of the capture.

I shall make every due enquiry, and be assured I will be attentive to you as far as my power and circumstances will admit.

From your letter I am led to suppose Colonel Fanning to be an officer commissioned by his Britannic Majesty, for the people who compose his force must be inhabitants of this State.

Since my return to this State, which is the same with the time of my being in my present office, I have received a variety of accounts of reciprocal violences and enormites between the well and ill affected to our government which disgrace humanity; but I have received no such information in such a mode as can justify my interposition; either as a civil magistrate or military officer, except in one case, on which I instantly took decisive measures. I have issued the most pointed orders against all rapine on any pretence, and against every act unbecoming brave and magnanimous soldiers and civilized people. I shall, as much as possible, attend to the strict execution of such orders; but for the grievances of which the people you mention complain, I can do nothing at present but put the judiciary power in vigor and preserve it free to hear the complaints of all persons, and independent to determine them agreably to justice and the laws of the State. For this measure is now in train, and if the people you mention are really aggrieved, the regular mode of redress will be open to them. If they be not citizens of this State, or of the United States, I suppose they must be objects of the law martial, which, so far as depends on me, shall be executed agreable to the usages of civilized nations. I cannot discover from your letter whether the Scotch gentleman you mention is a prisoner of war or a civil prisoner. Upon application made to me by or for him, which will enable me to distinguish, measures shall be taken suitable to their condition.

I am, gentlemen, your obedient servant,

THOMAS BURKE.

Without further comment on the above letters, we leave them to the perusal and reflections of the reader, and return to Fanning where we left him with his band of heroes at Wilmington, basking in the reflections of royal favor and inspirited by the tokens of that favor which he received to aim at still greater achievements.

BATTLE AT MCFALL'S MILL.

"They remained at Wilmington three days, during which time he received a commission from Major Craig, of Lieutenant Colonel, and a suit of rich regimentals, with suitable epaulettes, sword and pistols. He set out on his return to Chatham, and at McFall's mill, having encamped, intelligence was received by express that Colonel Thomas Wade; of Anson county, with six hundred and sixty men, were at Betti's bridge, on Drowning creek, twenty miles south of McFall's mill. The express reached the camp about eight o'clock at night. Fanning ordered his men to mount their horses and march immediately. At the dawn of day, ten miles north of Betti's bridge, they came up with Colonel Hector McNeill, having with him three hundred men; the whole number then amounted to three hundred and forty. Fanning took the command, and soon learning that Colonel Wade had crossed the bridge to the eastern side of Drowning creek, he turned to the right, and passed up a swamp to a crossway, expecting to find Colonel Wade between that swamp and the creek The crossway was distant about three-quarters of a mile from Betti's bridge Fanning halted at the crossway and gave notice of the order of battle. His men were directed to pass the crossway, two deep, and all having got over, Colonel McNeill was ordered to turn down the swamp to the left towards the bridge, to cut off Wade's retreat in that direction. He was ordered not to bring his men into action unless Fanning should be hard pressed and in danger of being defeated, but to watch the progress of the battle, and if Wade should be routed by securing the pass to the bridge, to prevent his retreat, and capture as many prisoners as possible- Fanning was to turn to the right from the end of the crossway with all the other men, and they were directed to follow him in the same order in which they passed the crossway, until he should reach the extreme left of Wade's line, when upon a signal to be given by him, they were to dismount and commence the fight. Eleven men were left to guard the crossway and prevent the escape of the horses, the swamp being impassible for miles except at this crossway.

"These orders being given, Fanning, preceding his column, passed the crossway, his men following him. As soon as he passed, he discovered Wade's men drawn up on the top of the hill in line of battle. The ground was favorable for his attack. There was no undergrowth of bushes, and the pines were thinly scattered on the slope of the hill. Fanning immediately perceived the injudicious position which Wade had taken, and confident of victory, rode on to the left of Wade's line. Before, however, he had proceeded as far as he had intended, one of his men was thrown from his horse, and in the act of falling his gun fired. Instantly Wade's line fired, and eighteen horses belonging to Fanning's men were killed. Fanning wheeled, gave the signal to dismount, which was instantly observed by his men, who poured in a deadly fire upon Wade's line. Fanning rode along his line in front and ordered his men to advance upon every fire, and they continued to advance and fire until they got within twenty-five yards of Wade's line, when it suddenly broke, and the men fled in the utmost confusion. Fanning pursuing with activity, and expecting that their retreat by the bridge would be cut off by Col. McNeill, he had no doubt of taking them all prisoners. To his astonishment, he found that Col. McNeill had not occupied the ground to which he was ordered; that he had passed down the right of Wade's line, only a short distance, and left the way to the bridge open. Fanning pressed on the fugitives, and soon took forty-four prisoners. He then directed a few of his men to mount, and with them he pursued Wade at full speed, for two or three miles. But Wade had fled at full speed, and Fanning could not overtake him.

"During this fight, as well as upon every other occasion, Fanning displayed the most daring courage. Dressed in rich British uniform, he rode between the lines during the fight, and gave his orders with the utmost coolness and presence of mind. It is strange that he had not been selected by some of Wade's men, as he was at the close of the fight, not twenty yards distant from them. He did not lose one of his men; only two or three were slightly wounded. As he ascended the hill, Wade's men shot over his, and when he approached the summit, Wade's men were so panic struck that they fired without aim. Wade lost 27 killed, and of the prisoners taken, several died of their wounds.

" The battle was fought about 10 o'clock in the forenoon, on the—— day of July, 1781. It is said that Wade had 600 men: Fanning fought the battle with 240 men, for the detachment under Colonel McNeill was not engaged. Orders were given for burying the dead, and the wounded were placed under the care of Fanning's Surgeons."

This was the first time that he had been engaged, at least when invested with authority, and, considered merely as a commanding officer, he certainly acquitted himself with honor. Cool and self-possessed every where, judicious in his arrangements, ready to expose himself when really necessary, vigilant and quick to perceive where an advantage might be gained, and prompt and energetic to avail himself of every circumstance or occurrence that could be rendered auxiliary to his success, he showed that, with proper intellectual training and moral culture when his character was forming, he might have made a commanding officer of higher grade and of much distinction, in a better cause too, and on a more extended theatre. We cannot do otherwise than feel some regret, both for his own sake and for the cause of humanity, that his character had not been formed under a better influence; but we must acknowledge the hand of an overruling Providence in the affairs of men.

" Among the prisoners taken was Joseph Hayes. He was recognized by Capt. Elrod, of Fanning's party. Elrod alleged that Hayes had plundered his house and ill-treated his family, and Hayes was ordered to be instantly hanged. The order was executed. Hayes, after hanging fifteen minutes, was cut down. One of the surgeons being present, thought that he could resuscitate him, and determined to make the trial. Perceiving the appearance of returning life, he informed Elrod of the fact, and Elrod told him to persevere. He did so, and Hayes was restored to life.

" In the evening Fanning set out on his return. During his march on the next day, an incident occurred which is worthy of being recorded, as furnishing some relief to the painful scenes which the country was then witnessing.

A scouting party apprehended Col. Thomas Dougan, of Randolph county, and brought him to Fanning. He had been sent by the Whigs of the upper counties to learn the situation of affairs on Drowning creek; the strength and position of the Tories; and their plans of operation. He was beloved by the people of his county, both parties regarded him as an upright man, and a friend to his country; and those who differed from him in opinion as to the contest in which they were engaged, abated neither their esteem or affection. With Fanning were several of his intimate acquaintances and personal friends. who all knowing that by the custom of the times, men taken under circumstances like his were immediately hanged, apprehended the same fate would attend him. They resolved to make a generous effort to leave him. Trials, often upon such occasions, were short and their execution prompt. Col: Dougan was brought forward, his case was heard in a few minutes, and Fanning ordered him to be *hung*. Dougan's friends interposed their entreaties, and whilst they were imploring Fanning to spare his life, he was mounted on a horse with a rope round his neck, and placed under the limb of the tree to which he was to be suspended. At this moment one of his friends, finding entreaties unavailing, told Fanning in peremptory terms, that if Dougan was hanged he would instantly shoot him. A general mutiny was threatened, when Fanning resolved to leave Dougan's fate to the decision of the forty men who had attended him in all his expeditions. They divided, and a majority declared in Dougan's favor. He was then taken down and treated as a prisoner."

"Another man, by the name of Johnson, from the same neighborhood, was taken either with Dougan or about the same time. He also was much esteemed, but not, by all parties, so much as Dougan. Elrod was a young man of true courage, and lived in the fork of the Yadkin. Although he committed many atrocities and was much dreaded in the country, he was capable of performing, occasionally, a generous act: but some further account of him and of his death; at which Dougan was present, will be given hereafter in a separate article.

"At Mc Fall's Mill, Col. McNeill and Fanning separated; the latter with his forty men; returned to Beck's Ford on Deep river, where his men dispersed, and part of them returned to their respective homes. The prisoners taken at Betti's bridge, with Col. Dougan "and others," were left with Col. McNeill, to be sent to Wilmington. "During the time Fanning remained in the neighborhood of Beck's Ford, Stephen Lewis and —— Short, who had deserted him on his march to Wilmington, returned to his camp. He reproached them for their desertion, and told Lewis he would put him to death; that his men must be true to him, as he intended to be true to them; that they were at liberty to punish him with death the moment he should prove unfaithful to them, as he would punish with death those who should prove unfaithful to him. Lewis treated his admonition as well as his threat with levity. Fanning raised his gun, and standing within a few feet of Lewis, took deliberate aim at him: his gun snapped; he then drew his sword and made a pass at Lewis' head, and cut him severely. Some of Fanning's men rushed in and prevented a repetition of the blow, and Lewis' life was spared. It was by such prompt, decisive conduct, and by a constant display of energy, firmness, and daring courage, that he sought to win the esteem and attachment of his men and such was his success, that many followed his fortunes who disapproved of his barbarous cruelties, being led on by their admiration of his extraordinary qualities—they thought him invincible, and that with a handfull of men he could defeat large detachments.

"Captain Robert Roper, of Chatham, collected a small party of Whigs and marched up Deep river to attack Fanning, who was still at Beck's Ford. Fanning seeing some of Roper's men on the opposite side of the river, attempted to cross the river, accompanied only by Short. As soon as they entered the river they were fired on and Short wounded. They retreated; and directing his men to mount and follow him, he hastened to a ford a few miles above, where he crossed; and being acquainted with all the paths and roads of the neighborhood, he went down the river along a small path, expecting to find Roper still at Beck's Ford. In this he was disappointed—Roper retired down the river in haste, and Fanning pursued him till late at night, when he abandoned the pursuit. He then had with him only twenty-three or four men. On the next day he proceeded down the river and took Moore of Hillsboro', a prisoner. He was an inoffensive man, and at the solicitation of one of his men, who was acquainted with Moore, Fanning paroled him. On the same day he took Wyat and Tomlinson prisoners, near the gulph on Deep river; and as they were connected with an active whig family, he resolved to hang them. They were placed in a cart with ropes around their necks. The cart was driven partly through a gate, to the top piece of which the ropes were about to be fastened, and then, when they were about to be swung off, some of Fanning's men who knew them interfered and saved them. He left their fate, as he had done that of Col. Dougan, to the decision of his followers. Fanning immediately set out for Wilmington, and took Wyat and Tomlinson on with him as prisoners, and delivered them to Major Craig.

"He remained in Wilmington five days. His camp was near the brick house at Belvidere. Here an incident occurred which marked the peculiar traits of his character. He sent three of his men to bring water. At the spring they met with some British soldiers; and owing to some difference with them, they were put under guard. Fanning was informed of this fact, and he immediately ordered three British soldiers who were in the camp to be put under guard, and gave notice to the officer who commanded at Belvidere of what he had done, and that he should retain those men until his were returned. The officer, indignant at his insolence, drew his sword and hastened to Fanning's camp. Fanning was lying in a tent, and the officer entering the tent, inquired whether he was Col. Fanning, who had dared to arrest and place under guard, three British soldiers. Fanning answered that he was the man. The officer raised his sword and made a pass at him, which Fanning eluded by his agility; and having grasped his sword as he rose, he pointed it to the breast of the officer, and swore he would run him through if he attempted again to lift his sword. The officer saw the danger which threatened him. They entered into conversation, which ended in a declaration made by Fanning, that he would retain the officer until his men were returned. A soldier was immediately despatched for Fanning's men, and upon their return to camp the officer and British soldiers were discharged.

CAPTURE OF COLONEL PHILIP ALSTON.

Immediately after his return he made his famous attack on the house of Colonel Philip Alston, who lived in the south-west corner of Chatham county, and in a bend of the river, on the north side; called the Horse Shoe. On his return from Wilmington, he encamped at Cross Hill, near the present town of Carthage, and on the place then, or afterwards occupied by Mrs. Glascock. There he received information that there was a party of men at Col. Alston's, and he resolved to attack them. Alston, with a good deal of the daring and reckless character about him, had been very severe on the Tories, especially during the early part of the war; and now, when Fanning seemed to be carrying every thing before him, and when no Whig in that region could feel safe in his own house a single night unprotected, he had more cause of apprehension than many others. He may, therefore, have had these men simply to protect his house from the depredations of these freebooters; but, according to my information, Fanning was informed that he was raising a body of men for the purpose of attacking him; and therefore he resolved to take him by surprise, and before he could be fully prepared even for defense.

Such was the reason assigned in McBride's papers for the attack on Alston's house; but I have recently received a communication from a correspondent who lives in the Scotch region, and in whose judgment and careful investigations I have much confidence, in which he gives, in substance, the following account: Colonel Wade, with a hundred mounted men had been through the region, watered by the tributaries of Drowning's creek and the Raft swamp, taking vengeance on the Tories for some injuries which he had lately received from them Among others, he made a visit to Kenneth Black, a man in comfortable circumstances, but a Tory; and not long after he left, Colonel Fanning came along, going South, with about a dozen Whig prisoners, among whom was a lawyer by the name of Lightwood. Fanning stayed all night at the house of his friend Black, and was very kindly entertained. Next morning after breakfast, he resumed his march, and Black accompanied him for a few miles, as a pilot. Fanning's horse had been so badly foundered that he was unfit to travel, and at parting, he and Black exchanged horses. When returning home, on the north side of Ray's mill creek, he met Colonel Alston, with a number of men. in pursuit of Fanning, and for the purpose of rescueing the prisoners As soon as he saw them he turned up the creek and attempted to escape on Fanning's foundered horse. They discovered and pursued him, shot at and wounded him: but he went on some two hundred yards farther, into the edge of the swamp, and then fell with his face on the ground. When they came up they smashed his head with the butt of his own gun, and when begging for his life.

Alston, finding that it was useless, did not continue the pursuit very far; but, on his return next morning, he called at Black's and told Mrs. Black how some of his men had killed her husband, for which he expressed much regret. Thence he went to a neighbor's house, where old Hector McNeill (not the Colonel,) and John Buchan were engaged in making the coffin. Alston had sold a negro woman to McNeill, but not having sold her husband with her, he had run away, and he accused McNeill of harboring him. He snapped a pistol two or three times at his head and then carried him off a prisoner, telling him that if the negro was not returned by such a day, he would hang him. Mrs. McNeill engaged her own negro man to catch the runaway, which he did; and then she, in company with another lady, took the negro home to his master, confined and guarded by her own negro man. Her husband was then released; and, as both parties viewed each other with distrust, Alston was probably confirmed in his former suspicion.

If I am not mistaken in the localities mentioned by my informant, the transactions above related took place in the south or south-west part of Moore county; and if so, Fanning at this time must have had his head quarters at or not far from Cross Hill, where I had always understood he had them, where he had got his prisoners is not known; but as Alston was endeavoring to rescue them, it is probable that they were from his region of country. Nor is it known to what point he was aiming to take them. My informant says, playfully, that he was taking them to his "Pravo" or "Caboos," in South Carolina; but we presume that he either took them to Wilmington, or gave them into the hands of some of his Tory friends who carried them away and delivered them to the British. He soon returned, however, and went to the house of Mrs. Black, where he was informed of all that had been done, and the facts, we may suppose, were feelingly described, with all their aggravating circumstances. When he learned that Alston had pursued him; that he had carried away McNeill as a prisoner; that he had killed his friend Black, who had received him so hospitably only a few nights before; that he killed two beeves for his entertainment, he became desperately enraged, and mustering all the force he could, set off forthwith for Alston's house. What number of men he had is not known; but, if he had not his full complement, they were increasing every day.

At this time, when flushed by so many victories, and confident of success, it made but little difference with him whether his enemy outnumbered him two to one, or was fortified as by the rocks of Gibralter. He only wanted to know that there was an enemy within striking distance, and he anticipated the victory as already gained. On receiving intelligence, therefore of the party at Alston's house, he immediately set out; and as the river had been a little swelled by a rain, he directed his course to the north-west for a few miles and then turned to the right, crossed the river at Dickerson's ford, three or four miles above Alston's, and went down on the north side. They arrived on the premises about day-break on Sunday morning, August 5th., and immediately commenced the attack. The sentinels being asleep were taken by surprise, and made prisoners. Those at the gate, on the opposite side of the enclosure, were fired on but not being killed or badly wounded, they ran into the porch where most of the other party were lying asleep. They too were fired on; but as soon as they could get into the house, the doors were fastened and all the preparation for defence was made that could be made at the moment. The windows were soon demolished; and many of the balls passing through the plank; killed or wounded the men inside.

The house was a two story framed house; and being weatherboarded, ceiled and painted, was one of the best houses then to be seen in that part of the country. It stands now just as it did then, with the exception of some additions, and still bears all the marks of war that it had when left by Fanning. On the west side was a large porch, one end of which had been made into a bed room, with a door opening into the hall, and this was the room usually occupied by Mrs. Alston and her husband. She now kept her bed, which was thought to be the safest place for her; and her two little children were put up into the chimney. This was done by putting a small table or bench in the fire-place for them to stand on, which was about as high as the front part, and thus they were entirely beyond the reach of the bullets.

A few rods from the house, on every side, was a strong rail fence: behind which Fanning posted his men and commenced a brisk firing, which was returned by the party in the house, and kept up, without much effect on either side, until after the middle of the day. There was among the assailants, a lieutenant from the British army by the name of McKay, or as, I am told, it was then pronounced and is now written, McKoy, who had either returned with Fanning from Wilmington, or, according to my authority, had been sent by Major Craig, probably for the purpose of observing the state of things in the country whence Fanning had taken so many prisoners, and being in Fanning's camp when the news came of the party at Alstons, he promptly joined the expedition.

Having been accustomed to the use of the bayonet and to a rush when a place was to be taken by assault, he became impatient at this mode of attack, which seemed likely to accomplish nothing, and he told Fanning that if he would give him the command he would take the house in a few minutes. Fanning promptly granted his request, and he as promptly entered on the execution of his purpose. As the plan was for all to rush up, burst open the doors and enter, *pell mell*, he started first and ordered the rest to follow him which they did without hesitation, and some of them *pari passu;* but as he jumped over the fence and alighted on the ground, a rifle ball entered his heart, and he fell dead on the spot. Most of those who had got over the fence or were still on it were more or less wounded, and they retreated to their former position behind the fence. Foiled in this unfortunate effort; and driven back with loss, the genius of Fanning, ever fertile in expedients, was now busy in contriving some way to accomplish by stratagem what he had failed to effect by force; and he first bribed a free negro to set the house on fire at the far side where it was supposed he could do it without being observed; but Alston having noticed Fanning talking to the negro, or seeing the negro go round, and suspecting his design, went to the window and shot him when in the very act of applying the fire. The negro was not killed, but severely wounded. During all this time only one or two had been killed in the house, and four or five wounded; but Fanning's loss in killed and wounded was more than double. After the failure of his plan with the free negro, an almost incessant fire, on both sides, was kept up for some time, but still without much effect; and through the whole of this fierce conflict thus far, Mrs. Alston had been in her bed and had remained unhurt, though the weatherboarding and ceiling were riddled with the bullets, which remain to this day as they were then; and some of them must have passed not more than two feet above her when she lay in the bed.

After such a protracted conflict and with so much loss to himself, Fanning began to feel discouraged; and either from the apparent hopelessness of his cause, or from an apprehension that the report of the guns might alarm the country and bring a Whig force upon him too great for his strength, he was on the point of abandoning the enterprise and drawing off his men, when he or some of his men fortunately discovered a large ox cart in the barn yard, a few rods in their rear; and with this he resolved to make his last effort. He ordered them to fill it with hay or straw, and bring it up, intending to set it on fire and run it up to the house. If he could burn the house they would be obliged to surrender, and his end would be accomplished.

Several of the men promptly volunteered their services; the fire was brought; and they were about ready for the operation. The plan was to run up the cart with its load, tail foremost, and thus keep it between them and the house, so that the bullets could not reach them. Alston, perceiving their design, and knowing well, that defended as they would be by the cart, it would be impossible to shoot them, concluded that their only chance was to capitulate; but how was it to be done? The men all believed that, if any of them ventured to go outside of the house, instant death would be the consequence, though the flag of peace were waving over their head; and if Alston himself went out, no matter under what circumstances, or who might be with him, he would be picked out and made the first victim. In this perilous and critical moment, Mrs. Alston came out of her bed room or stood in the door; and with perfect composure, requested them to commit this business to her. At first, the men all objected, and particularly her husband, who thought it very improbable that Fanning, under all the circumstances, would respect even a lady of her standing, though a wife and a mother, and bearing the sacred emblem of peace; but, as she insisted on it, they finally consented. A man may brave danger with deliberate courage, like a hero on the field of battle, where all the intense excitements of the conflict, and the hope of victory are bearing upon him; he may meet death with a kind of defiance, like a savage or a desperado; he may die with tranquility like a patriot, or with resignation and hope, like a Christian; but such serenity of mind, such calm and entire self possession, such mild and dignified firmness in moments of sudden and extreme peril, when life or death is seen to depend both on what is done and how it is done, is peculiar to woman. Mrs. Alston, raising a white flag, opened the door and went out on the step, where she paused for a moment to see if she could discover any indications of the treatment which she might expect to receive.

As soon as Fanning saw her, he called to her to meet him half-way, which she did; and then, in a calm, dignified and womanly manner, said to him:—"We will surrender, sir, on condition that no one shall be injured; otherwise we will make the best defence we can; and, if need be, sell our lives as dearly as possible." Fanning, who could sometimes respect true courage, whether in man or woman, promptly agreed to the proposal, and honorably kept his word. The men all then surrendered and were immediately paroled.

In the papers of Judge Murphy, as given in the University Magazine, it is stated that during the fight, Capt. Andrews, a British officer, who had accompanied Fanning from Wilmington, having climbed up the fence that he might shoot with more effect through a window of the house, as he stood on the fence, one of the men in the house shot him through the head; and I have stated that Lieutenant McKay, from the British army was killed. As these accounts are all traditionary, an exact agreement in every particular is hardly to be expected; but in this case both may be true. There may have been a Captain Andrews and also a Lieutenant McKay present, as officers from the british army, both of whom were killed; for such was Fanning's success at this time that it would not be at all strange if two or more of the British officers should be with him on any occasion of the kind; and then there were more killed than we would gather from Judge Murphy's account. Next morning after the fight, eight were buried on the brow of the hill, a few rods from the house; and whether any of the wounded afterwards died of their wounds, I have not learned, but, probably they did. Most of the dead were of Fanning's party; for only two, or at most three, of Alston's men were killed. According to the statements which I have received, Alston had a little over twenty, and Fanning somewhere about thirty men; but Judge Murphy says that Fanning had only twenty four men including Captain Andrews, and that

twenty-six men surrendered to him. I have no disposition
to question the correctness of this statement, but it seems
a little strange, that with such a disparity of numbers in
their favor, Alston and his party, even if driven to extrem-
ity by having the house set on fire, should be unwilling
to meet their enemies in open combat. My information
was obtained partly from the papers of Mr. McBride and
partly from Dr Chalmers, who now lives in the house
which was then occupied by Col Alston. In addition
to the reports or traditions of the neighborhood, Dr Chalmers, two or three summers ago, traveled with his family
through he State of Tennessee and became acquainted
with the sons of Col. Alston, from whom he got a statement of the whole transaction. Col. Alston, himself, lived
only a short time after the war, having been killed as I
was informed by a negro whom he had treated with severity or provoked in some way: and the children were probably too young at the time to have, in after life, a very
distinct recollection of the scene; but they must have often heard the facts related by their mother. John Spears,
who lived down the river, and was wounded in Alston's
house, when he returned urged Captain Cunningham,
who had a company of Whigs then under his command,
to pursue Fanning; but he declined; and Judge Murphy
says, that according to report, "a company of Whigs under
Capt. Duck were lying near Alston's house and heard the
firing from the morning till evening and feared to come
to Alston's relief.

CAPTURE OF CAMPBELTON, NOW FAYETTEVILLE.

The fact is that the very name of Fanning was at this
time quite appaling, and he was regarded by all in that region, Whigs and Tories, as almost invincible. So far as
my recollection serves me, I do not recollect to have heard
of an instance, during the summer of 1781, in which the
Whigs showed a willingness to meet him with an equal,
or any thing like an equal number of men; but, within
the entire range of his operations, no effective resistance
was made, and the country was really in his power. I
have always understood that, during this period, the summer and fall of 1781, he had about eighty men who were

either constantly with him or at his bidding, and whom he could at any time summon to his presence in a case of emergency; that he seldom had less than thirty or forty, and that when Colonels McNeill and McDougal, united with him, they could muster from three to five hundred strong. In the high career of successful adventure, and with flattering prospects before him, it appears to have been his object to take as many prisoners as he could for the British camp, and to bring the country into subjection to British authority. He seldom murdered any, except such as had proven treacherous to his cause, and those who had excited his wrath by uttering threats or by resisting his progress. When excited, so impetuous and vindictive was his temper, that whoever had given him the least provocation, if in his power, was sure to be made the victim of his malice, and in all cases the process was a summary one.

A few days after he captured Col. Alston, and his party, he and his confederates took possession of Campbelton, now Fayetteville, and carried off Col. Emmet, Captain Winslow, and other leading men, prisoners; but the best and perhaps the only authentic account which we now have of this transaction, is contained in the following letter, furnished by Governor Swain, and published in the University Magazine, March, 1851.

Col. Emmet to Gov. Burke.
"Campbelton," 19th. *August,* 1781

"Sir:—I am under the disagreeable necessity of informing your Excellency that on Thursday last, the 14th. inst., between nine and ten o'clock in the morning, this town was, in the most sudden manner imaginable, surprised by a party of the enemy, under the command of Colonels Slingsley, Ray and McNeill. They entered the town in so sudden and secret a manner that it was out of the power of any man who was in it to make his escape. I was at a plantation I have about a mile off, when I was alarmed by a party of about twenty horse. The noise of their horses' feet just gave me time to slip into a swamp where I lay until the party left the plantation, which they did as soon as they had deprived me of my horses. I then got over the river, when I learned their numbers to be about three hundred. I was likewise informed the same evening, that McNeill, with one hundred men, had gone up the River on the west side, and, not being able to judge where they might intend to cross the river, thought it my best way to keep where I was. Had I done so, I might have kept clear of them, but at such times so many reports are flying, that there is no such thing as distinguishing the true one. At midnight, between the 16th and 17th, word was brought me that a Col. Fanning came down the country with *one hundred and eighty men*, made a short stay at Cross creek, had crossed the river at lower Campbleton late in the evening, and at that time was encamped, with an intention in the morning to pursue his march up the river, and so join McNeill on the east side. On this information, I unfortunately crossed the river, early in the morning, and about nine o'clock was taken a prisoner by McNeill, on his return to town.

"It was not my intention to trouble your excellency with this tedious relation, by way of intelligence. I am sure you do not expect it from one in my situation, but as I have many private enemies in this county who would be glad to lay hold on any circumstances to vilify my conduct and blacken my name, I have taken the liberty to trouble you with this, by way of vindication.

With all deference, I remain, sir,
Your Excellency's obed't serv't,
JAMES EMMET.

To his Excellency, Thomas Burke, Esq., Governor of N Carolina"

Let the reader now go back a little and observe the boldness and rapidity with which all the above victories were achieved. Besides the almost daily capture of some influencial individual who would be acceptable to the British as prisoners; the cutting off of such as were particularly obnoxious to him, and the dispersion of small parties of armed Whigs, on the 15th. of July he entered Pittsboro', and captured all the officers of court, with most of the principal citizens, whom he delivered in a few days to the British authorities at Wilmington; on the 5th. of August, he captured Col. Alston and his party in his own house; on the 14th. he took possession of Campbelton and made prisoners of the principal citizens; on the 1st of September, the battle was fought at McFall's Mill, on the Raft Swamp, where he gained on his part an almost bloodless victory; and on the 13th, he entered Hillsboro', and captured Governor Burke, with his whole suite and thirty or forty of the prominent citizens. This was perhaps his most famous exploit— the one which spread more alarm over the country than any other, and is the only one of his important achievements which remains to be described.

CAPTURE OF GOVERNOR BURKE.

With whom the project of capturing the Governor of the state and delivering him to the British at Wilmington, originated, is not known. Perhaps it never was known to more than two or three, nor is it a matter of much consequence in itself, but the enterprise was one of so much boldness in its conception and so much energy and heroism in its execution, that the traditions of the country have ascribed its paternity to Colonel Fanning. From some circumstances however, while he was the most prominent and efficient actor in the whole process, I am disposed to attribute its origination to some other. The movement was one of peril and of bold adventure; it necessarily involved the loss of many valuable lives on both sides; it was successful beyond any reasonable expectation; and therefore, being vastly important in its results to the whole community, deserves to be traced, if possible, from its inception to its consummation; but in doing so, we are left very much to conjecture, and in that sphere every one must think or judge for himself. If it was not proposed by Major Craig at Wilmington, which we think very likely, it was probably first suggested to Colonel Ray, or some one of the Scotch leaders, by the following incidents, which were rather of an amusing character, and which occurred only a few days before they began to assemble at their place of rendezvous. *The race is not to the swift, nor the battle to the strong*, is a maxim of the highest authority, and we see it as often vivified in military operations as in other pursuits.

As the Tories, now stimulated by the proximity of a British force and by the daring achievements of Fanning, were more menacing and troublesome than they had been at any time since the battle of Moore's creek, Colonel

James Hinton, of Wake county, with about two hundred and fifty men, crossed the Cape Fear and penetrated into the north side of Cumberland County, for the purpose of subduing or dispersing them. John McLean, who, I have been told, had been a Captain in the Tory army and was still a loyalist, but not so zealous in the cause as some others, lived on the north side of upper Little river, on one of its tributaries, and his mill was known to be a place of resort for the Tory corps that were embodying in that region. Hinton went to McLean's first, but was disappointed in not finding his enemies. However, as they were in pretty good quarters and supposed they had no cause to apprehend any danger, they were in no hurry to get away. The captain was not there to receive his visitors and treat them with the best he had; but they concluded that they would make free and "Johnny Penny like," help themselves to whatever they preferred. Some of them cut down corn for their horses and others turned theirs into the field. They killed a beef or two, got some other articles of provisions, and in fine spirits, commenced making preparations for dinner.

About the same number of Tories were at no great distance, embodied under McLean, McDougal, Malcolm McKay and Archibald McKay; but they were some eight or ten miles above, near the mouth of Jones' creek. Having got some intelligence of Hinton's visit in the neighborhood and wishing to approach him very cautiously, instead of taking the ridge road, which was much the nearest and best, they followed the meanderings of the river, and near the Beaver ponds, captured Barganier and Gholson, then on their way to join Hinton. An old man of that neighborhood, by the name of William Kennedy, followed his Tory friends, whether for the purpose of joining them or for some other reason, is not now recollected; but he took the ridge road, which was much the nearest, and when he got there, instead of finding his friends, as he expected, he found the place occupied by a crowd of strangers. As the men were all out, some attending to their horses and others occupied in different ways, he saw nobody in the house, and walking through the kitchen door, he asked the old negro woman, Saph, who those men were? but she replied, rather equivocally, "They are your own country people." With much haste and agitation, he repeated the question two or three times; but always got the same equivocal answer. On seeing some of the Whigs approaching, and being perfectly aware of his danger, without some device, he stepped out quickly into the open space before the door, and clapping his hands with great earnestness, exclaimed at the top of his voice, "Clear yourselves or you will all be taken prisoners! Clear yourselves for Colonel Fanning is coming round the field with five hundred men! Clear yourselves or you will all be surrounded and taken prisoners! Clear yourselves!" From his manifesting so much earnestness and so much apparent concern for their safety, they could hardly doubt his good intentions, and they had no time to parley or reflect. Mounting their horses in haste and telling him to come along, they galloped away over the bridge and in much confusion. He did not object to go with them; but he must first get his horse. After crossing the bridge and finding that Kennedy was neither with them nor following them, they began to think there was no danger and some of them returned to search for the man who had given such a false alarm; but he had got what he wanted, an opportunity to escape, and was not to be found. The Whigs encamped for the night a little above the bridge; but had not entirely recovered from their panic: and their circumstances required circumspection, for they could not, with two hundred and fifty men, encounter an army of five hundred, with Fanning at their head, and in their own country, where they were all acquainted with the swamps, and where they might, in a few hours, be reinforced by a much larger number.

In the course of the night the Tories arrived, but found no Whigs. One braggadocio blustered much, and was quite distressed because the Whigs were not there—"that they might give them such a drubbing;" but old Daniel McPherson thanked God that they were gone. Early next morning, sentinels were placed at the bridge. These sentinels, on seeing two or three men, who when hailed, said they were for the country, fired on them. This gave the alarm at the house and they all marched in battle array down the hill and over the bridge, but still they found no Whigs; for, becoming apprehensive, it seems, from the firing of the sentinels, that Fanning, with five hundred men, was close at hand, they had mounted and fled in haste to the Cape Fear river. They crossed at a ford called the Fox Islands, and encamped for the night a little above Col. McAlister's. The Tories followed them to the river, but did not cross. Next morning the Whigs went up the river to the cross-roads, about half a mile above Atkin's ferry, where they halted for refreshment, and placed sentinels at the river, just above the ferry. They killed two beeves and some sheep, turned their horses into a fine pasture, and were preparing for a good feast. Some were roasting their meat, on spits before the fire, and some had begun to eat, when the Tories fired on the sentinels across the river; and directly a dozen guns were fired. Becoming alarmed again, they mounted their horses and fled, some leaving their meat roasting on spits before the fire, and some leaving both the bread and meat, which they were eating, just lying on the ends of fence rails. They had a few Scotch prisoners, chiefly men and boys—such as Hugh Ochiltree, John McLean, from Indian branch, and his son Neill, Malcom McPhail, Malcom Graham, Archibald McLean and a few others, about a dozen in all. As none of them were men of influence, and as there was no time for delay, they just left them at the river, and without giving them any orders or instructions what to do. The Whigs, after getting into the Raleigh road, about half a mile, drew up across the road and made preparation to receive their enemies; but their prisoners, finding that they had been so unceremoniously left behind, began to consult among themselves whether they had better return home, remain there, or follow their captors; but it was finally concluded that if they returned home, the Whigs should they come back again at any time, might accuse them of breaking custody and treat them with severity; and that they had better follow on and stay with them, at least until they knew what disposal was to be made of them. With this intention they all set off together; but the men under arms, on seeing their heads through the bushes, as they were ascending the hill in front, supposed them to be their enemies in hot pursuit, with Fanning at their head, and again fled in much confusion

After going seven or eight miles, they took up the camp for the night; and next morning, as the ten days for which the men had engaged, were expired, they were all disbanded and returned home, except Captain Hadley's company, which continued up in that direction, and was at the battle of Cane creek. The conduct of the Whigs on this occasion, is not to be attributed to cowardice, but to the alarm which they got at McLean's, and from which they had not yet recovered. Their conduct is still made the subject of much amusement in that region; but without due regard to the circumstances. We all know, how often men under arms become mysteriously or unaccountably panic struck, and utterly unfit for any manly exercise of their powers. This often happens with veteran and well disciplined soldiers, but much oftener with militia. These men had left home with little or no camp equipage, and without any other arms than such as they carried in their hands. Having engaged for only ten days, they regarded it as an excursion of pleasure rather than as an enterprise full of toil and peril. Expecting to capture or disperse, in a few days, all the Tories they could find, they never thought of meeting with any serious opposition. When they found themselves in the midst of enemies, with an armed force at least equal in number to their own, within a few miles, who were probably increasing every hour, and who, instead of avoiding, were seeking for them, the case was altered, and they were compelled to take care of themselves; but when they learned, or were led to believe, that an armed body, of at least double their number, with Fanning at their head, were in pursuit, alarm was unavoidable, and their own safety became the paramount object. The panic into which they were thrown by the crafty old Scotchman only showed the terror of Fanning's name; and was very much like many others which were produced about that time, by the mention of his name. This whole affair was, however, an unimportant one in itself, and would hardly deserve our notice, but for the bearing which we suppose it had on the expedition to Hillsboro. It was well calculated to increase the courage of the Tories; and as the way was now clear, it might readily have suggested to some of them the thought of making a bold push immediately into Hillsboro, and carrying away the Governor. This was somewhere about the first of September, though the precise date is not recollected; and on the fifth, five or six hundred of them, according to tradition, had assembled with their leaders, on the "Dry Fork," a tributary of Crane's creek, and were ready for marching orders. Much the largest body of Tories was now assembled, that appeared in arms at any one time after independence was declared; and, according to tradition, they considered themselves as the prime movers in this enterprise. They certainly were the principle agents, and the greatest sufferers. The flower of the Scotch population were in this embodiment; and all their best officers, most of whom had been much in the British service, and in all of whom they had full confidence were at their head.

Colonel McNeill was there, and had the command of the whole. It belonged to him, according to military use-age, as the senior officer; but it would have been conceded to him, out of respect as the oldest man, for he was now advanced in life and had the full confidence of all who knew him. Colonel Duncan Ray, young, talented and enterprising, was also present; and Colonel McDougal, though he was not made Colonel until afterwards, and then held no higher rank, as I am told, than that of Captain or Major. These had all been much in the British service, and had the unlimited confidence of their countrymen. Fanning may possibly have been the originator and the master-spirit of this whole enterprise; but he was not with them when they were assembling; nor when they commenced their march. Tradition says that he had the separate command of his own corps, and merely co-operated with them, acting on his own responsibility and as occasion required. Governor Swain, in his communication to the University Magazine, or rather Judge Murphy, says that when Fanning and McNeill united for the purpose of striking sudden and effective blows, at remote and effective points, they commanded alternately day by day; and this, we may suppose, was sometimes the fact, especially in the early part of their career, before Fanning had got much experience, or had attained much celebrity; but, according to the most reliable traditions I have heard, it was not a general or frequent thing; for, I am told, that the Scotch would not fight under him, nor be commanded by him. They disliked his character, and all the better part of them abhored his atrocities. In those days, 'tis said, they would not fight under any other than a Scotch commander; and, on this occasion, they merely co-operated with him for the purpose of accomplishing the object. He was, no doubt, the life and soul of the business, and gave energy and success to the whole movement. His courage and military tact, which would have made him a prominent character anywhere, now gave him the *virtual* command; and gained for him, in public estimation at least, the honor of the achievement. Leaving "Dry Fork," the place of their rendezvous, on the morning of September the 6th, and keeping their plans concealed, they commenced their march up the country and, receiving some small reinforcements as they advanced, Colonel Fanning joined them on or near Deep river. With the moral power of Fanning to urge them on, their movements were rapid and they met with no resistance from any quarter.

So far from dreading any effective opposition, they were determined to fight their way, and actually cut off or routed the only collection of men who, by spreading the alarm and serving as a nucleus for an ingathering of Whigs, could have given them any trouble. History, I believe makes no mention of the skirmish at Kirk's farm; yet it was quite a spirited affair, and is worthy of record. Captains Allen and Young, of Orange county, encamped for the night on Kirk's farm, on the east side of Haw river, and near east creek, where they were as they supposed, many miles from any tory force, and were apprehensive of no danger. Whether they were out on a voluntary excursion, or had belonged to Colonel Hinton's corps, which had been disbanded only a few days previous and were keeping together for mutual safety, until they could get into a stronger Whig neighborhood, we have not learned; but they were only twenty or twenty two in number. They were attacked by about twenty five or thirty; and as they were taken a little by surprise, the result was what might have been expected. Fanning who appears to have been remarkable for the facility and accuracy with which he got information respecting every thing within the range of his operations, did not deem it necessary to go himself, but sent off a detachment under the command of Captain Richard Edwards. With characteristic boldness and rapidity of movement they came up just as the day was dawning, and killed the sentinel a man by the name of Couch who had been posted at the end of the lane, then retreating a short distance to a thicket, where they lay in ambush and awaited the movements of the other party. The killing of the sentinel gave the alarm at the house, and the party marched out under Captain Allen to give them battle, or rather to ascertain the cause of the alarm, when the Tories emerged from their concealment and a severe conflict ensued, in which some important lives were lost on both sides, and others mortally wounded. Allen and Young were both severely wounded; the former recovered, but the latter died of his wounds within a few days. Captain Edwards was killed on the spot; and ten were left dead on the field. Nearly a third of the whole number engaged were either killed or wounded; and some of the latter died of their wounds within a few days. I have given the main facts in this affair as I found them in McBride's memoranda; but that the assailants were a detachment from Fanning's corps, I infer from the following facts. It was just at the time when they were on their way to Hillsboro', and was a very little off their route; it was not more than four or five days before the battle at Cane creek; and the detachment was commanded by Richard Edwards, who was then a captain under Fanning. There were then in Fanning's corps three brothers by the name of Edwards—Richard, Edward and Meredith; and two of them are known to have been in the skirmish at Kirk's farm. When Richard was killed, one of the others, Edward we believe took the command; and he is said to have been killed the next week at the battle of Cane creek. We simply state the facts, and leave the reader to form his own opinion.

The capture of the Governor was one of the most remarkable feats of the Tories during the war, and one of the most memorable events in North Carolina. "On the first of September the battle was fought at McFall's Mills, on the Raft Swamp, and on the 13th, about daylight, Fanning and McNeill entered Hillsboro', the seat of Government, by different roads, seized Governor Burke, his suite and other prominent persons, and proceeded with their usual celerity towards Wilmington." Having entered the town in opposite directions and by the dawn of day, before any body was apprised of their coming, they were enabled to take nearly every man they wished; but their first object was, of course, the Governor and suite. The jail guard finding that Governor was captured and perceiving their own danger; assumed the badge of their enemies, by substituting oat straw in their hats for their deer tails, and thus attempted to ride through the Tories in the streets; but Fanning recognized them at once and cried out, "The rebels! the rebels!" then rushing upon them with the fury of a tiger, he broke his sword on the steel plate in the cap which was upon one of their heads.

Having secured the Governor and all the prisoners they wanted, some of them engaged in drinking and robbing the stores. After plundering the town, their next move was to break open the jail and release the prisoners, but to remain long there was neither policy nor interest; and as Capt. John McLean did not drink, the prisoners were committed to his charge Some of the men who engaged in plundering the stores became so drunk that they could not get away and had to be left behind. The Whigs then rallied, and they were taken prisoners.

Among the prisoners were William Kinchen and Col. John Mebane; but Col. Alexander Mebane, made his escape by leaving a very valuable horse to the care of the enemy, and taking it on foot through the high weeds which had grown up very densely in the cross streets. Then returning to his home and friends, in the congregation of the Hawfields, with all the haste he could, he spread the alarm among the Whigs, and collected as many of them as could be got together on the spur of the occasion. General Butler who lived on the west side of the congregation near the place where Judge Ruffin's mill now stands, being notified, came and took command of the men. A much larger number might have been soon rallied for the rescue of the Governor; for that was one of the strongest Whig neighborhoods east of the Yadkin; but as Fanning was so notorious for the boldness and celerity of his movements, whatever was done had to be done with the utmost despatch. Having ascertained that the party with the Governor and suite in charge, were crossing the river and intended going down on the west side as the nearest and most expeditious route to the Tory region, their object was to get before them and occupy some favorable position. The ground at John Alston's mill, a little above or below what is now Lindley's, appeared the most suitable, and there they made their stand.

The number engaged on either side is not known with any degree of certainty, but according to the best traditionary accounts, or those which seemed to be most worthy of credit, the Tories had about six hundred and the Whigs about three hundred a little more or less. The Scotch say that they must have had about six hundred, for they had five hundred at the place of rendezvous in the lower side of Moore county, and after they commenced their march they received two or three accessions, of which Fanning's corps was one; and we can hardly suppose that to have consisted of less than fifty or sixty. The night before the battle, old Colonel McNeill, who seems to have had the exclusive command, at least of the Scotch, on this expedition, had a presentiment, or what he regarded as a presentiment, of his death. We say nothing here about the reality of such impressions, nor, if real, about the source from which they come; but his was by no means a solitary case of the kind. Officers of high standing in their profession and of undoubted courage, have often had, on the eve of a battle, such a presentiment or impression of their approaching fate as to become depressed in spirits and comparatively inactive.

Several such instances occurred on both sides, during the revolutionary war, and with men who could not be charged with idle fears or superstitious notions. Col McNeill, on this occasion, felt constrained to disclose the state of his mind to some of his friends who tried to laugh or reason him out of his sombre mood, but in vain. The brave old Hector who had witnessed more appalling scenes than the one now before him and had stood firm when a thousand deathful balls were flying around him, quailed when summoned, and so distinctly, as he supposed, to appear in the presence of his Maker, that there was no possibility of escape. He was not a man however who would bear the charge of cowardice, nor would he shrink from what he considered his duty on such an occasion.

It was known that the Whigs were gathering and that they might expect a conflict in the course of the day; but precisely when and where was entirely a matter of conjecture. In the morning, old Hector like Ahab, King of Isreal, when going up to battle at Ramoth Gilead laid aside his regimentals, and appeared at the head of his men in disguise, clothed in a hunting shirt and other parts of dress corresponding, very much like a common soldier; but his time was come and his destiny could not be changed. No disguise could conceal him from the eye of the Omniscient one and no artifice could countervail his unerring purposes. It is easy for him to conquor by many or by few, and whatever may be the resources or apparent advantages of one over another, he controls every thing and gives the victory to whom he pleases.

As the Tories were crossing the creek, and advancing through a hollow or strip of low ground, along which the road led, the Whigs, from the brow of the hill, on the south side of the stream, gave them a deliberate fire. and with tremendous effect. They were taken very much by surprise, and quite a number were killed and wounded, as they approached the stream, and before any danger was known or apprehended. Captain McLean halted his men in the rear and they all sat down to rest. On hearing the first fire of the Whigs, Governor Burke, and most of the prisoners jumped to their feet and looked about; but the Captain told them to be quiet; for if they attempted to escape they should every one be shot down; and they had to obey. Colonel McNeill, on seeing so many of his men cut down by the first fire, and perceiving that if they continued to advance, it would be at a great sacrifice of life, ordered a retreat; but McDougal cursed him, and asked him if he was not going to face his enemies—"Was that the encouragement he was giving to his men?" The order was then countermanded, and they attempted to proceed.

At the next fire of the Whigs, five or six balls entered the Colonel's body, and he fell dead on the spot. So did several others, and many more were wounded. When he fell, some one thoughtlessly cried out, "The Colonel is dead." "It's a lie," exclaimed McDougal, in a bold, strong voice, "Hurra, my boys, we'll gain the day yet." His death was very prudently concealed, for many of the Scotch declared afterwards, that had it been known at the time, they would not have fired another gun, but would have sought for safety in any way they could. At this juncture, the principal officers got together for hasty counsel, or for the purpose of agreeing on some one to take the command; but those highest in office all refused, and they seemed to be at their "wit's end." At length, some one said, "Perhaps McDougal will take the command;" and instantly every eye was turned to him, if not "imploringly," at least with a strong expression of assent. He accepted; and nobly did he meet the responsibilities which he had assumed. According to the traditions in this region, when McNeill fell, the command devolved on Fanning, of course, as the one next highest in office; but the traditionary accounts of the Scotch are different; for, according to them, they would not be commanded by him, and he would not be under any other. He was therefore regarded merely as a co adjutor, responsible only to himself, and having the command of none except his own men; but with them, as it appears, he actually did more, in a few minutes, to make an impression on his enemies, and arrest the tide of success, than all the rest effected with their veteran officers and military tactics, during the whole of the action.

Amidst all this, success on the part of the Whigs, and all this disaster and confusion among the Tories, Fanning contrived to cross the stream at another place, or to ascend the hill at another point, and, by making a little circuit, attacked his enemies in the rear. Being thus taken by surprise, the Whigs were thrown into momentary confusion, but quickly recovered; and, for a short time, the contest was fierce and bloody. Nearly every Whig who was killed during the action fell at this time, and in the course of ten or twelve minutes. The charge of Fanning was furious untill his arm was broken by a rifle or musket ball, and he was carried off the field, when the next officer in rank, we suppose, took the command. Probably, it was on seeing this havoc made of the Whigs by this manœuvre of Fanning's, and viewing their situation as now desperate, considering the disparity of numbers, that General Butler ordered a retreat, and commenced it himself. The men, in obedience to orders, were following his example, when Col. Robert Mebane got before them, and by arguments and remonstrances, so far inspired them with his own heroic spirit that enough of them returned to renew the battle and keep the ground. It seems to have been at last a drawn battle; for neither party claimed the victory, and neither appears to have kept the ground for any length of time. The Tories were glad to get away with their prisoners, and the Whigs became willing to let them go. A few years ago, an old Quaker friend, who appeared to have been well informed on this subject, and whose powers, though he was then about fourscore, were unimpaired by age, told me that Col. McDougal, after he took the command, came, under great excitement, and—to use his own language,—"in a foam of sweat," to the house in which the prisoners were then kept, and took an oath that if the Whigs did flank him, as they were trying to do, and drive him to extremities, he would put his prisoners all to death, before he would suffer them to be taken from him. Whether this determination became known to the Whigs at that time, and had any influence in causing them to give up the contest, my informant could not tell; but if they were apprised of it, we presume, they would prefer that their friends should remain prisoners, than that they should be shot, *en masse*, by their captors. At all events the battle appears to have ended by mutual consent, and both must have left the ground about the same time. The tradition among the Whigs, has been, that they kept the ground, and the tradition among the Tories, is that they kept it; but neither could claim it on very decisive evidence; and as the Whigs slowly withdrew or slackened their fire, the Tories, glad to get away, moved off with their prisoners towards Wilmington.

Very little was known about the battle at Moore's creek, at least by the present generation, and very little was said about it, until recently. Within two or three years, some of our ablest men have given it their attention; and since the facts have been brought to light, it is regarded as one of the most important events during the war. If some one who is competent to the task would undertake it, and fairly ascertain the facts in relation to the battle on Cane creek, it would be found that there was quite as much military tact and courage displayed as at Moore's creek; and, in propotion to the whole number engaged, there was certainly much more bloodshed and destruction of life. A more bold and deliberate act of courage is hardly on record than was done by Col. Robert Mebane in the hottest of the battle. In the midst of the conflict with Fanning, when the Whigs must have been nearly between two fires, as the Scotch were advancing up the hill, they got out of ammunition and Mebane walked slowly along the line, carrying his hat full of powder and telling every man to take a handful, or just what he needed. The day was warm, the 14th of September, we suppose, and near the middle of the day, as the battle commenced about 10 o'clock; and by wiping the sweat off his face with his hands, after handling the powder, when he got through, his face was nearly as black as the powder itself. The precise number of killed and wounded is not known, and cannot be readily ascertained; but it was rather larger, in propotion to the whole number than was usual in battles of that period.

Neither Whigs nor Tories really kept the ground and attended to the burying of the dead; but next morning the neighbors met there and buried thirty-two in one pit,

Besides these, according to the concurrent tradition of both parties, many of the dead were carried away by their friends and buried in the neighborhood. Of the wounded, some of whom could get away themselves and others were carried away by their friends and acquaintances, a number are known to have died of their wounds, soon after. Between the foot of the hill and the creek, the dead and dying were strewed about in every direction, and some of them were lying in the water. One of the Scotch companies, the one under the command of Capt. Archibald M'Kay, had six killed on the grounds and twenty-six wounded; some other companies suffered equally as much and hardly any of them escaped entirely. Some of Fanning's men were killed; but he was so repaid in his movements and made such havoc wherever he went that his corps suffered less than the others. The Whigs, too, lost many, and some valuable lives; but, according to their traditionary accounts, not so many, even in proportion to their number, as the Tories. A friend, in writing to me from the Scotch region, says, that "including all of both sides who were slain on the field, and all who died soon after in consequence of their wounds, the number could not be much under a hundred;" and this estimate, which looks quite reasonable, taking everything into view, we suppose to be not far from the truth.

Several of the highest officers on both sides were killed and nearly an equal number of each. These were men of much merit as officers, and their death was a great loss to their respective parties. On the Whig side Major John Nalls and Colonel Lutteral were among the slain. In the Scotch traditions I find that Nalls has the rank of Colonel assigned to him; but I have never heard him called, in this region, any thing but Captain or Major Nalls; and as the latter seemed to be more frequently applied to him than the former, I have given him that title. He was killed near the close of the battle by a Tory who singled him out with his rifle and shot him dead on the spot. Having done so, and seeing three of the Whigs sitting on their horses at a little distance, whom he mistook for his own party, he galloped up towards them, and as he approached called out, "I have just killed Major Nalls;" but the words were hardly out of his mouth until three pistol balls entered his heart, and he fell dead. Nalls left a widow and family of young children. On every account he was much esteemed in Chatham county where he lived; and as an officer he was highly valued. Vigilant, enterprising and rapid in his movements, he was dreaded by the Tories. Colonel Lutteral was also killed about the close of the battle and was a great loss to the country. He is said to have been a brave and valuable officer; but his men thought him too severe in his discipline; and this may have given rise to a tradition in the neighborhood of the battleground that he was killed after the battle was over by a Whig., a man by the name of Frazer. According to this account, he rode back after both parties had gone away, to look over the scene or to ascertain the number of killed and wounded. On seeing Frazer, then the only man on the ground and mistaking him for a Tory, rode up and fired at him with his pistol but without effect. Frazer then leveled his rifle and shot him thro' the body. He did not fall at once, but rode to a house, something like a mile off, where he lived only a few hours, and was next day laid in the burying ground of a neighboring church. The Tory account is more plausible, because it is corroborated by other circumstances, and is as follows. Having advanced at the head of his men within pistol shot of a Tory from Randolph, by the name of Rains, who was in the act of loading his rifle, and fired at him with his pistol, but without effect. He then wheeled his horse, and dashed off, to get out of reach before the other would be ready to fire; but Rains, having finished in time' levelled his gun at him, when at full speed, and shot him through the body. He did not fall, but rode to a house about half a mile distant, where the good people took him up stairs and furnished him with a bed and every comfort in their power. While lying there, bleeding and dying, he dipped his finger in his own blood and wrote his name upon the wall. The house stood there as a Monument of the Cane creek battle and of Colonel Lutteral's death until about seven or eight years ago; and the Colonel's name retained its freshness and brilliancy until the last. There were two men belonging to Fanning's troop by the name of John Rains, father and son; and McBride says that John Rains Sen., was killed at the battle of Cane creek. If it was he who killed Nalls the accounts would be consistent; and it is possible that the Scotch while they have correctly preserved the facts have unwittingly confounded the names.

On the Tory side, two officers in Fanning's corps are known to have been killed, John Rains and Edward Edwards. The latter had been a lieutenant before, as we infer, and took the place of his brother. Richard, who was killed at Kirk's farm, the week before. It is probable that he still commanded the same company or troop at Cane creek, and there met the same fate. Of the Scotch division Colonel McNeill, the veteran soldier and the brave officer, fell at the second fire; and the promising and much beloved Colonel Dushee Shaw lay at his side. He was a mere youth, but seemed to have all the manliness of mature age. Modest and unassuming, but firm and sagacious, polished in his manners, heroic in his spirit and chivalrous in his bearing, he was the very idol of his friends and there was great lamentation for his death. They left thirty-one of their number on the ground, who were too badly wounded to be removed; but they were nursed and cared for, some by the neighbors and some by their friends from a distance, who came and stayed with them until they died or had sufficiently recovered to go home. Among the wounded who were thus left, was Malcolm Downey, whose sister Mrs. Neill Murphy, walked all the way up to Cane creek from Robeson county, some seventy-five or eighty miles, and nursed him until he expired. She was the mother of the Rev Murdoch Murphy, deceased, and the Honorable John Murphy, late Governor of Alabama. Other instances of a similar kind might be related; but we will let one suffice for many. Such women deserve to be remembered and to be held up as examples of firmness in times of peril, and of devotedness to the cause of suffering humanity.

At such a time, no respect is paid to a man's opinions however honestly entertained; and but little allowance is made for his inoffensiveness or inactivity in the cause which he approves. Force is everything, and wherever that can prevail, conscience and everything else is disregarded. There were two brothers by the name of James Torry and George Torry, who were Tories, and had been with the Tories previous to this battle, but their brother David Torry, was a Whig, and had hitherto staid at home. At length, however, he was taken prisoner with Hugh Laskly, and they were both in a manner, forced to join this expedition to Hillsboro', at least they were induced to do it against their judgment and all their principles of patriotism, rather than be sent to the prison ships at Wilmington, and they were both among the wounded at the battle of Cane creek, but whether both or either of them died I have not learned. Probably there were other cases of a similar kind, but such compulsory measures, which are an intolerable hardship, belong exclusively to a state of civil war.

A Tory who was mortally wounded in the battle gave his watch to the miller on condition that he would bury him when dead; and the miller fulfilled his promise, but a brother Tory, on learning that the miller had the watch went and took it from him. Another of the Tories was found dead next morning, about a quarter of a mile from the place of action, on his feet or apparently supported by his feet, and leaning against a tree, but without any wound that could possibly have caused his death. It was generally believed that he had died of fright; but his death might have been occasioned by apoplexy, an affection of the heart, or somthing else.

On the evening of the battle, or very soon after, a lady by the name of Lindley, wife of Simon Lindley, was shot dead in the road by some one lying in ambush, and it was believed to have been done by her own husband. Some Whigs happened to be near enough to hear the report of the gun, and led by a curiosity or a suspicion that something was wrong, came up immediately to see what it meant. The lady had a child at the breast, and when they found her the child was trying to suck. That child was afterwards removed to Howard county, Indiana, and has left a large family. So strong was their suspicion of Lindley's guilt, that some of them instantly went in pursuit and soon took him prisoner. They brought him to a house which was close by and set one of their number to guard him for a short time, until the rest could determine what they would do with him. It was rather suspected, though there was no proof of the fact, that the guard had given him an opportunity to run, and he took through the orchard between J. Newlin's and William Johnson's. However, the alarm was given and the rest all ran round the house to see what was the matter. One of them shot in the direction pointed out by the guard as the one which Lindley had taken, and killed him without seeing him. The load of shot struck an apple tree, and one of the shot glancing off, perchance, struck Lindley in a vital part and killed him on the spot. It was believed that he, having become apprehensive that she would betray him, had waylaid her and killed her; but he having been killed so soon after, without any investigation of the case, it was impossible to ascertain the truth by any ordinary process. Such is the tradition of the neighborhood.

The most cowardly are the most anxious to be thought brave; and those who least deserve honors are the most proud of them. At the commencement of the battle, there was a man present from the immediate neighborhood, by the name of —— who was an arrant coward, but who had, not long before, got the office or the title of Captain conferred upon him. Whether it was real or only nominal, I did not learn. Probably it was a kind of militia appointment by his Tory neighbors; but he was so proud of it that for some time he had made his wife always call him *Captain*. As soon as the action commenced he became very much frightened and took to his heels. Two or three Whigs pursued him and would have overtaken him, if he had not suddenly disappeared in a way which seemed to them rather mysterious. Near the mill was a long, high rock which, at the lower end, terminated in a precipice some twenty feet high. At the base there was a shelving under, or a recess of some kind, which made a very comfortable hog bed in the winter, and in which a man if fairly ensconced there, could not be seen except from the ground on one side. As this was the only direction he could take, or the only one in which the danger would not be as great as where he was, he took the rock and two or three whigs pursued him to the far end, when he jumped down the precipice and disappeared. His pursuers went to the edge of the precipice and looked down, then off on every side without getting a glimpse of him; and, concluding that it was not worth while to spend time in the search, they returned to the scene of the conflict. In the afternoon, when he thought the danger was over, he went home, and entered the house with a very distressed countenance looking pale, and so weak that he could hardly walk. His wife, with surprise and alarm, said to him, "why, *Captain*, what in the world is the matter with you, that you look so bad?" "O," said he, "don't call me Captain any more. I am a poor wounded man, shot through and through, and the blood is running desperately." Of course she ran up to him in perfect fright, and began to open his clothes, in order to see the wounds, and do what she could for him, but to her great mortification, she soon found that it was not *blood* and that was the end of his military career, as effectually as if he had been shot through the heart.

A friend in the Scotch region, the son of a very respectable Whig officer during the war, writes to me that, as he has been credibly informed, he thinks the Tories had two brass cannon at Cane creek; but owing to the advantageous position of the Whigs, they could make no use of them until they got on the high ground. If they had cannon, it is probable that they had captured it with the Governor in Hillsboro'; and such I believe is the traditionary account.* By the desperate attack which Fanning made on the rear of the Whigs, such a diversion or confusion was produced that the Scotch at length got up the hill; but they had been so roughly handled and so many of their best officers and men had been either killed or wounded, that they were more anxious to get away than to fight; and the Whigs tacitly, though reluctantly, consented to let

*The following song, which was made by some one of the corps, not long after the battle, was sent to me by my correspondent in that region, so often alluded to already, who says that he wrote it down as it was repeated to him, not long since, by an aged Whig. It corroborates the suggestion made awhile ago that the cannon were taken from Hillsboro'; and the tradition that they were thrown into Lindley's mill pond, may be true. At all events, it deserves some attention; and it is to be hoped that a thorough search will be made.

"The Governor and Council in Hillsboro' sought,
To establish some new laws the Tories to stop;
They thought themselves safe, and so they went on with their show,
But the face of bold Fanning proved their overthrow.
We took Governor Burke with a sudden surprise,
As he sat on his horseback and just ready to ride;
We took all their cannon and colors in town,
And formed our brave boys and marched out of town;
But the rebels waylaid us and gave us a broadside,
That caused our brave Colonel to lie dead on his side;
The flower of our company was wounded full sore,
'Twas Captain McNeill and two or three more.

The Captain McNeill who is mentioned in the song as having been wounded, was Captain Neill McNeill, from upper Little river, in Cumberland county.

them go. When they drew off from the scene of conflict they turned to the east and kept down the stream until they came to what is now known as Lindley's mill; where a few of the Whigs having rallied, they had another little skirmish, and to get clear of an incumbrance, they threw their cannon into the pond, where it is supposed, they might yet be found if a proper search were made. Expedition was a paramount object with them; for a little delay would give the Whigs time to rally, and in such numbers, that they could not only rescue the prisoners, but take them too. As they had engaged in the expedition not to fight, unless it was unavoidable, but to capture the Governor and as many of the most active patriots as they could, victory was no object any farther than it was necessary to secure their retreat. It was therefore necessary to disencumber themselves of everything that could impede their march, and to act altogether on the defensive. They had made a fine haul and had got a number of 'big fish. Their great concern now was to get them safely delivered to the British authorities in Wilmington; and for this purpose they would either fight or run as circumstances might require. This would surely recommend them to the King, and when the rebels were subdued, give them a pre-eminence in the country. A defeat by the Whigs, any encounter with whom was not sought but dreaded, would have blasted all their hopes and been a source of intense and enduring mortification

A few of the Whigs a dozen or twenty in number, did make some show of resistance on the evening of the battle or next morning, at a' place a few miles below and not far from the foot of Hickory mountain; but they were so few that they were soon dispersed, and after that the way was clear. They soon got over deep river, into the Tory region, where nearly every man was rejoiced at their success, and was ready to lend them a succoring hand and bid them God speed

PURSUED BY GENERAL BUTLER.

It is stated in Wheeler's history of North Carolina that "General Butler endeavored to intercept them with a *superior* force, and did so at Lindley's mill on Cane creek, where an engagement took place on the following day." I presume the author had some good authority for the statement, and I would be glad had he given it, for my information has been different, and if that was wrong I would like to have it corrected. According to my information, the battle was not at Lindley's mill, but at old Jack Alston's, a little above, when the Tories arrived at Lindley's mill on their retreat, a few of the whigs had rallied there and a small skirmish ensued; but it was only a little brush on their rear or their flanks. Now if General Butler had a superior force in the engagement on Cane creek why did he not gain the victory. He had the advantage of the ground, and he was not, like the others encumbered with prisoners or any thing else. To suppose then that having these advantages, a superiority of numbers, a more eligible position and freedom from any encumbrance while his enemies were inferior in number, occupied an unfavorable position and had a large number of prisoners to guard, after all he let them get away with their prisoners; would be disreputable to General Butler and to the men, who fought so bravely on that occasion, or if by some untoward occurrence, they did elude his grasp in the first engagement, as he was superior in numbers and unencumbered, why did he not pursue them and intercept them at some point below—Perhaps my information has been wrong, but according to the most reliable accounts which I have always had from both sides, the Tories outnumbered the Whigs at least two to one, and I recollect no conflict of the kind during the war in which there was more real bravery displayed or which reflected more credit upon the Whigs than the one on Cane creek, except, perhaps, the one at Ransour's mill, and if the Tories on that occasion had been commanded by such a Tartar as Colonel Fanning, or if he had been there at the head of his Saracen corps with his daring courage, his rapidity of motion and his quick perception of whatever advantage might be taken, the result would probably have been very different. I have been thus particular in my account of the battle on Cane creek, one of the most important events in Fanning's career and one of the most calamitous to the country,—with the hope that some one who is competent to the task will take it up and give it a more thorough investigation.

It has been stated that when old Col. Hector fell in the battle, some of the officers denied that he was dead, probably making the men believe that he was only wounded; and, for the time being, they put McDougal in his place. After leaving Cane creek, in order to keep up the delusion, they appointed to the command another of the same name, Hector McNeill, son of Archibald and Jennet (Ban). Having afterwards lost an eye, he was known in subsequent life, by the name of "one eyed Hector," but at this time, as he had not yet lost his eye, he appears to have filled the place quite respectably. From Cane creek, they went directly to their head-quarters on the Raft Swamp, and after crossing Deep river they stayed all night at the house of Mr. McRae, father of the present Collin McRae, Esq., who gives the following account of their visit: "My father lived on Deep river. My Mother's maiden name was Burke. When the Governor of that name was taken prisoner at Hillsboro,', by Fanning and his company, they stopped at our house all night on their way to Wilmington. The Governor was put into an additional apartment, at the end of the house and there closely quartered. Our bag of meal was seized and cooked immediately; and, having been previously robbed, my mother had no bed clothes, except one cotton sheet, which was carefully wrapped around my infant brother, John, by his mother's side. One of the company seized hold of one corner of this sheet and continued to jerk and shake it until the infant rolled out on the floor. By way of retaliation, my mother made some attempts before day to let her namesake, the Governor escape, but without success."

The Governor appears to have been treated with as much courtesy, and to have had his situation made as comfortable on the road as could be expected. After leaving Cane creek a few miles, and finding that the Whigs were not pursuing them, Capt John McLean, who had the prisoners in charge, dismounted and asked the Governor to ride his horse. He replied, "I am your prisoner, sir, and must expect to fare as a prisoner" but McLean insisted, and the Governor mounted his horse. The Captain then took it on foot but soon obtained another horse. Capt. Neill McFall, or, according to the Scotch orthography, McPhaul, lived on the Raft Swamp, and kept a mill. His house was head-quarters for the Tories all over that region and was the place of rendezvous before and after every expedition in which the different corps united. When they arrived at McFall's with the Governor, the prisoners were all given in charge to Colonel Ray, and a detachment of men sufficient for the purpose was assigned him. He conducted them to Wilmington and delivered them to Major Craig; but most of the men remained at McFall's. In a few days before Colonel Ray had returned with his detachment, and after Fanning, with his corps, had left, they mustered three hundred strong and were drilled by Colonels McDougal and McNeill, on the plantation now owned or occupied by Mrs. Bethea near Floral College. This is another collateral proof that the force with which they encountered the whigs on Cane creek, has not been overrated on a former page; and that the conflict, which these patriotic men had to maintain on that momentus occasion, was something more than mere play.

Word had been to Major Craig, probably by express, that they had succeeded in capturing the Governor, with a number of other prominent Whigs, and that they would be there by such a time. A troop of cavalry was sent out to meet them and escort them back to town. A few miles below Elizabethtown, about Hammond's creek, they were met by this troop, and as they were approaching, Governor Burke said to the officers and men around him, "Now, gentlemen, I am Your prisoner. Heretofore I had hopes of being released, and, therefore, I did not feel like a prisoner; but now I feel that I am indeed your prisoner." He had hitherto entertained the hope that General Butler would overtake them, and be able to effect his rescue; but was sadly disappointed. General Butler did pursue them, and probably with an augmented force, for, as the Tories out numbered him on Cane creek, it was very natural that, when about to pursue them, he should increase his strength by hasty drafts, or by volunteer companies; and a few years ago, the writer became acquainted with one or two and respectable men, in Caswell county, who were with Butler on this expedition, but had not been at the battle. It is not at all unlikely, therefore, that at this time he did have a force superior to that of the Tories; but he did not overtake them and never had a regular engagement with them. According to the traditionary accounts in that region; he was taken by surprise one night and made a hasty retreat. Colonel Ray, after remaining two or three days in Wilmington to rest and refresh his men, was on the return home with his detachment when he came upon Butler's camp, on Hammond's creek, while they were all asleep, and fired upon them. A few were killed, probably the sentinels, and some others were wounded. Such an attack, made with spirit and in the dead hour of the night, took them by such a surprise that they sought safety in the best way they could. A few evenings after, he had a skirmish with another body of Tories, and some British troops. This was quite a spirited affair for a short time but was soon over. General Butler ordered a retreat after the first fire, under a mistaken apprehension that the enemy had artillery, of which he was destitute; but Col. Robert Mebane, who belonged to his command, rallied as many men as he could and continued the conflict. Colonel Thomas Owen, father of General Owen, and of the late Governor Owen, was there, and, as General Owen informed me, took the chief command. The two colonels made quite a manly resistance for a while, but were overpowered and compelled to yield the ground. The whole affair was one of small importance, and the circumstances are not well known. Whether it was owing to the want of good generalship or to some untoward occurrences, we do not know; but the Governor was not rescued, and the expedition was not signalized by any important achievement.

With his laurels all fresh upon him and greatly increased by his recent exploit, as soon as his prisoners were safely delivered, or carried beyond the reach of their pursuers, Fanning returned to his old range, and pursued the same course of rapine, murder and devastation. During the last three months, his movements had been rapid; his plans bold and daring; and in every conflict he had come off victorious. Few men, with the same amount of force, have ever accomplished more in the same length of time; but after the British were driven from North and South Carolina, and after the army under Lord Cornwallis had surrendered to General Washington, at Yorktown, the prospects of the loyalists here, as well as everywhere else, became more and more gloomy, and their operations, if not less atrocious, were neither so bold nor so extensive. Fanning, however, had a considerable number who followed his fortunes and adhered to him with great fidelity to the last. With these, he was a terror to the whole country; for as his fortunes waned and his prospects darkened, he became more vindictive and more of the cut-throat assassin. Generally he kept his head-quarters on the south side of Deep river, and about Cross-hill, where he was in such a Tory region that he felt secure from any sudden attack of his enemies; but sometimes he had his camp on the north side of the river, and when he and his men were not out on some expedition, they employed their time in horse-racing, gambling, and such sports as were most congenial to their dispositions. The place where he had his camp for sometime, on the west side of Chatham county, and not far from the present residence of Doctor Chalmers, is still known by the name of *"Fanning's race paths;"* but we presume that no gentleman, with even a moderate share of honorable feeling, however much he might delight in the amusement of the turf, would not think of using them for that purpose! From the last of September, 1781, until some time in the summer of 1782, a great many murders and atrocities were committed by Fanning, or by his orders, along Deep river and for some miles on the north side, the dates and minute circumstances of which cannot be now ascertained. Many have been forgotten, or rather have not been sought for by any one who was competent and had leisure or opportunity to write them off, and throw them into the common stock of public information; for they still exist in the traditions of the country; and enough might be obtained to make a moderate sized volume of pleasant reading, at least for the young people of the country, at their fire-sides in the long winter evenings. We shall therefore relate a few of these, and give the best account of them we can, but without dates or chronological order, except in one or two instances, of deep and abiding interest, in which we have been fortunate enough to obtain the date from letters written at the time, or shortly after, by persons who were eye-witnesses of what they related, or had authentic and certain information.

MISCELLANEOUS DEEDS OF ATROCITY.

In the fall of 1781, and while Fanning still had a respectable number of followers, Captain John Coxe, who was a firm Whig, and who lived, if I mistake not, in the North side of Cumberland county, not far from the river, went up into Chatham with a small company of men, and took up camp for the night at the house of a man by the name of Needham. Fanning having been informed of this movement by some of his friends, went in pursuit with his whole corps and arrived there before midnight. Having tied their horses in a thicket, at a little distance from the house, they rushed up and fired on Coxe and his party before they were properly aware of their danger, or could make any preparation for defence. As none of them were killed, however, they all broke and run without their horses, or any thing else except their guns, which, in those times, every man who had taken up arms at all in defense of his country, always kept in his hand when awake, or by his side when asleep; but fortunately a part of them, in taking their course from the camp at random, happened to run by the place where Fanning and his party had tied their horses; and with great alacrity and promptness, they all helped themselves to horses, each one taking, without leave or license, the first horse he could get, as, they say members of Congress now take hats when leaving a President's levee; and they all made tracks a little faster than they could have done on their own stumps.

On the second day after this occurrence, Fanning and his whole troop went down to John Coxe's house and encamped there for the night. Next morning they plundered it and burned it to the ground, and destroyed every thing else on the premises that was destructable. John Coxe of course, kept out of the way himself but sent a messenger privately to his father, informing him of all that had happened. From this scene of desolation, Fanning with the whole of his banditti, went to the house of the old man Coxe, for a similar purpose; and when they arrived on the premises John Coxe, William Jackson and Robert Loe were at the house; but they heard the sound of the horses' feet, or got some intimation of their coming in time to make their escape, and they were fortunate enough to get away with so much adroitness, or in such good time, that neither Fanning nor any of his men, with all their vigilance and sagacity, had any suspicion of their having been there. Thus left, they had free scope for their rapacious and burning propensities, without let or hinderance; and they were not slow to improve their time.

While they were thus engaged, John Coxe and his comrades, who were still lingering within a short distance, as if unwilling to abandon every thing to their enemies or perhaps wishing to witness what was done, so that if the time of retribution should ever come, they might know what to do, agreed that they would go back as near as they could for safety, and while they kept themselves out of harm's way, might be able to see what was doing; but their curiosity, or an over confidence in their own activity, led them a little too far. Men who were engaged in a work so atrocious and had made themselves so odious to the community, were obliged to be always on the lookout, and always prepared for any emergency. While the most of them were engaged in burning and plundering, a few were off at a little distance, as sentinels, looking and listening in every direction; and either hearing a noise, or getting a glimpse of these men, they gave Fanning notice. Instantly he and a few others mounted their horses, dashed off in pursuit, and soon overtook them. When they came in sight, the three men fled in as many different directions; and Fanning with one of his men, pursued Jackson, who ran towards the Juniper. The other man shot first and wounded him in the back. Fanning then fired and broke his arm; but the ball passing through the arm, entered his body and he fell dead. Robert Loe took a pathway up the ridge; but Stephen Walker, one of the most cruel and blood-thirsty men in Fanning's whole corps, pursued him and, having overtaken him about a mile from old Coxe's house brought him back. Fanning ordered him to be shot, but as he was not killed by the first fire, he pulled out his own pistol and shot him dead. One of the men followed John Coxe, who aimed for the low grounds of McLinden's creek; but when his pursuer had got near enough to shoot and was just in the act of shooting, his horse stumbled and fell to the ground. By the time the horse had recovered sufficiently to continue the pursuit, Coxe was out of sight; and by this fortunate occurrence his life was saved. Robert Loe had been one of Fanning's corps; but for some reason or other, not known to the writer, he had left him and joined the Whigs. Knowing from the character of Fanning, what would be the consequence if he was ever taken, he ought to have been more guarded and not to have put himself under the very paw of the lion, but he showed no more rashness than was then common in the country; for such is the effect of familiarity with danger that people become reckless; and his fate was not very different from that of many others.

According to the traditions of the country, this Stephen Walker was a man of most unenviable notoriety, a perfect ruffian, a cold blooded murderer, who had no feelings of humanity, no sense of honor and no respect for moral worth. Many years ago, I was told by an old man in Randolph, that, making an excursion one night for the purpose, he shot a Baptist preacher dead in his own house in the presence of his family and when begging for his life, without any sort of provocation or pretext, except that the preacher was a Whig and had used his influence, which was considerable, in favor of independence. This is only a specimen of his atrocities; and no wonder that his name was a terror wherever it was known.

CAPTURE OF JAMES HARDING.

If a man's character is tested by the presence of danger, his wisdom is evinced by avoiding the stratagems and counteracting the plans of his enemies. Both are necessary in war and especially in such a civil war as raged for some time in this country, when a man's foes were often his nearest neighbors and sometimes even those of his own house; nor is it easy to say which is the most important or the most worthy of admiration. Sometimes, the one is especially called for and sometimes the other; but we feel the highest gratification, and are most hearty in our commendation, when we find them both combined in the same man. We had then many such in our country, of every rank, from the commander-in-chief down to the humblest citizen; and as every one ought to have the credit which he deserves, when we find such a man, however humble his station, we take a pleasure in giving his name to "the historic muse." Nine or ten years ago an old gentleman who had spent all his life in the neighborhood where the occurrence took place, and who had some recollection of those times, gave me in substance, the following account. There lived at this time, on the south side of Deep river and near the mouth of Bear creek, a man by the name of James Harding, who was a Whig and a man of a fearless spirit, bold in his address, frank in his manners and very prompt to use his tongue or his hand as occasion required. Of course, he was the more obnoxious to Fanning, who had sworn that, if he ever got him in his power, he would take his life; and, being aware of this, he was usually on his guard; but it so happened one day that a scouting party, when ranging through the neighborhood, unexpectedly came upon him; and taking him prisoner, carried him to head-quarters. He showed no apprehension of consequences and no unwillingness to go with them; but his captors were rather surprised to find him as sociable and pleasant as they could wish. They expected nothing else, and they thought that he could expect nothing else, than that he would be put to death as soon as they got to camp, yet he was serene and cheerful.

On entering the encampment, Fanning was much gratified with their success and with the thought that he now had it in his power to exterminate one whom he regarded as a hateful if not a formidable enemy. Harding, however, did not give him time to *do* any thing nor even to say what he intended to do; for he knew all that beforehand; but, walking up to him, with an air of perfect *nonchalance*, took him by the hand with much apparent cordiality and told him how glad he was of having an opportunity of joining his standard. He told Fanning that it had been his wish for some time to leave the Whigs and come over to him; but that no opportunity had occurred before of doing it with safety. Now he had got there and he hoped he would not be a drone in the camp. Fanning looked him full in the face all the time; but notwithstanding his sagacity and his skill in reading the countenances of people, he could detect no insincerity, either in the tones of his voice or the expression of the eye. So well did Harding act his part, and so complete was the deception which he practised, that Fanning gave him a friendly reception and a cordial welcome. From the first, he made as free with the men in camp as if they had been bosom friends and boon companions all their life. He joked with them, eat and slept with them, and in every respect, they were all Jack fellow alike.

By a similar course of familiarity and apparent frankness, he effectually conciliated Fanning, who laid aside every thing like mistrust or reserve, and made him a kind of confident. In fact, from his known character for boldness and enterprise, they all felt rather proud of the fancied acquisition which they had made; nothing was concealed; and no suspicions were harbored. If his feelings were harassed by the recitals of their murders and house-burnings among the Whigs, he kept it to himself; and all seemed to be perfectly smooth and right. Of the morals and religious character of Harding we know nothing; but whatever they were, he no doubt felt that he was in the hands of a man who had little claim on him or any body else for truth and fairness. He knew well that with such a man as Fanning when the object of his sworn vengeance was before him, an open, manly course would be certain death; and he probably thought that if he could foil him with his own weapons, and by any stratagem effect his destruction, or impair his strength, he would be diminishing the sufferings of his country and doing so much to aid the triumph of freedom.

Accordingly, when he found that he had Fanning's confidence, he remarked to him, as they were speaking of some meditated excursion, that he could put him on a plan by which he might capture a company of Whigs on the other side of the river, at the same time mentioning what company it was, or who was the captain; but he said it would be necessary that he should go over first and make the arrangements, by getting their consent to meet him on a given night and at a particular ford on the river, which was, of course, well known to Fanning: when he had made the arrangements he was to return to camp and conduct them to the place. Fanning, pleased with the proposal, give it his sanction; and, not suspecting any trick or unfair play, mounted Harding and sent him off with his usual benediction. When he met with his Whig friends, he made an arrangement with them very different from that which his Tory friends expected. They were to lie in ambush on the next night and near a specified ford on the river. A signal was agreed upon, which was so simple as not to excite the suspicion of Fanning or his men until Harding could get out of their reach; and, on giving the signal, they were to rush upon their enemies. The ford, being only a neighborhood ford, was a little rocky and difficult to cross. The banks were steep, especially the one on the north side; and the way was so narrow that not more than two could ride abreast. Having made his arrangements, he returned to head quarters and found all right.

His account of matters was satifactory, and at the proper time they all set off, Fanning and Harding in front and all in good spirits. They arrived at the river about the appointed time and took the ford. Some had crossed and were on level ground; some were plodding their way among the rocks; and some were ascending the bank. Harding then gave the signal and was answered by his friends to let him know that they were there. At the same instant he dashed toward them and fell into their ranks, when they all rushed forward and poured a heavy fire on their deluded enemies. All was confusion, and for a moment the utmost consternation prevailed. Such a scene as followed can be better conceived than described; and I shall leave it to the imagination of the reader. Suffice it to say that several were killed and a number wounded.

Among the slain or mortally wounded, was Stephen Walker, a man who was abhorred by every body except Fanning and his party; and at whose death, at least all the Whig community rejoiced. Fanning himself had the good fortune to escape, and the greater part of his corps; but he had never been so outwitted and discomfitted before. He never had been so mistaken in his man, nor so completely duped; and he never had met with any thing in all the battles and rencontres in which he had been engaged, at least since he had been a British Colonel, that so mortified his pride, or that so much imparied his military strength and his martial prowess. The precise number of killed and wounded I did not learn; but I understood that the Whigs lost none. Fanning and his party, I think, did not pretend to fight; for they were overpowered by numbers and were taken at such a disadvantage, where there was no chance for them all to get together, and on ground where they could not possibly form into any order, for either an aggressive or a defensive effort, all they could do was to seek safety by flight, and find concealment in the surrounding darkness.

In reading anything of the narrative kind, it adds much to the gratification when we can trace the order of events and see the connection of one with another, but in this and many other cases that cannot be done. Such have been the peculiar circumstances of this country, that incidents of the most interesting kind were left unrecorded until the dates and all the peculiar circumstances are forgotten. My informant believed that the above transaction took place late in the fall of 1781; but his recollection was not so distinct that he could be certain. It has been suggested to me that Harding made the arrangement with Colonel Gholson; and that the Colonel killed Walker with his own hand; but of this I have as yet had no reliable information. The main facts are believed to be correct; and it is a matter of so much interest in itself we hope, that as Colonel Gholson's descendants are still living, some in that region and some in the west, the circumstances will be more fully brought to light, and the transaction be fairly represented.

EXCURSION UP DEEP RIVER.

The reader will no doubt feel surprised, as the writer has done, to find that Fanning still kept the field and pursued his course of devastation with unabated zeal for months after the cause in which he was engaged had become desperate. After the British had left this state and had been driven out of South Carolina; after the British army under Cornwallis had surrendered at Yorktown, he still maintained as bold a front as ever, and fought on with an unyielding pertinacity. It seems strange, " 'tis passing strange," that in view of all these circumstances and when he had probably not more than twenty or thirty men; when confidence was reviving in the breasts of the patriots and when the paralysing effects of discouragement were pervading the ranks of the royalists, the Whigs did not rally in sufficient numbers to cut him off or capture him at once, and thus put an end to his murders and devastations; but whether it was owing to the terror of his name, or to the fact that they could not overtake him, none of the companies, so far as I have heard, that went down so often below Deep River to subdue the Scotch ever encountered Fanning. This was not all; for we find him at this time writing to Gov. Burke, with as great an air of independence and conscious dignity as if he had been Cæsar or Napoleon Bonaparte, and charging the Governor with murdering three of his men, dictating terms of peace and threatening to retaliate tenfold if reparation were not made and a stop put to proceedings. The occasion of this singular correspondence may be learned from the following communication of Judge Williams to Governor Burke.

Hillsboro, 27th Jan., 1782.

Dear Sir,

*   *   *   *   *   *   *

During this term seven persons have been capitally convicted, to-wit. Samuel Poe, for burglary, Thomas Ricketts, Meredith Edwards, Thomas Eastridge, and Thomas Darke for high treason; Thomas Duke and William Hunt for horse stealing. And as I suppose some application may be made for mercy, I have thought proper to represent to your Excellency the true point of view in which the several persons condemned stood before the court.

Thomas Darke, a captain of Fanning's and one of his right hand men, is the principal person convicted. He has been very active and enterprising, and near as dangerous a person as Fanning himself, and from his proved inhumanities and cruelties in cutting, hacking and wounding his prisoners, had acquired among those of his own party, the name of "young Tarlton."

Thomas Ricketts, though indicted of treason only, it is hard to mention a crime of which he is not accused and I have good reason to believe not wrongfully, murder, housebreaking, robbery &c., &c., are on the black list of his crimes, to which is added a general bad character.

Meredith Edwards and Thomas Eastridge were also indicted for treason. They are both men who appeared to be equally popular among the Tories, and very active, and men of Fanning's gang, though generally kind and humane to prisoners while in their custody, and seemed much to lament the fate of their particulr neighbors, whom they had taken with Governor Burke, and to express some uneasiness at seeing them in captivity. As to the general moral character of these men, it seemed to be pretty good, only great Tories—Eastridge from the commencement of the times.

* * * * * *

I have the honor to be, dear sir,
Your very obt' hum. servant,
John Williams.

From this it appears that several of Fanning's men had been captured, when, where, or by whom, does not appear; but after trial in the civil court, they had been found guilty of the crimes laid to their charge. Summary justice was then the order of the day, and three of them had been executed. This provoked the wrath of Fanning, and gave rise to the following very characteristic letter from him to Governor Burke.

Feb. 26th, 1782.

Sir:—I understand that you have hung three of my men, one Captain and two privates, and likewise have a Captain and six men under sentence of death.

Sir, if the requisition of my articles do not arrive to satisfaction, and the effusion of blood stops, and the lives of those men saved, that I will retaliate blood for blood, and tenfold for one, and there shall never an officer or private of the rebel party escape that falls into my hands hereafter, but what shall suffer the pain and punishment of instant death. I have got your proclamation, whereas it specifies this, that all officers or leading men, persons of this class guilty of murder, robbery, and house burning, to be precluded from any benefits of your proclamation, for there never was a man who has been in arms on either side, but what is guilty of some of the above mentioned crimes, especially on the rebel side, and them that's guilty is to suffer instant death, if taken. If my request agreeably to my articles ain't granted, and arrive by the eighth day of March next, I shall fall upon the severest and most inhuman terms imaginable to answer the ends for those that are so executed, and if the request is granted immediately, send a field officer to Deep river, to Mr Winsor Pearce, and there he may remain unmolested, or to Colonel Phelon Obstones,, under a flag, till we can settle the matter. So no more, but I am in behalf of his majesty's troops,

Your most humble servant,
DAVID FANNING.

Commander of the Royal Militia of Randolph and Chatham.

P. S. On Friday, the 7th. of January last, I wrote to Lawyer Williams the terms that I was willing to surrender under, and he wrote to me that General Butler would not comply with my terms till he had the approbation of the Governor. On Wednesday, the 11th inst., the flag was to meet me at a certain house with the letters, and as the flag was coming it was waylaid by Charles Gholson and a party of men, from which it appeared to me that they seemed more like taking my life by treachery than coming upon peaceable terms; but as the gentleman that bore the flag, Balsom Thompson, acting so honorable to his trust, the moment he arrived at the place, he let me know of it, and declared himself innocent, which gave me grounds to think he would act with honor still.

On the 15th of the present, Mr. Williams, Mr. Clark, and Mr. Burns, were the gentlemen that were kind enough to wait upon me with a blank parole and letter, that my request was granted by the Governor. In the meantime, the gentlemen waiting on me at the place appointed, there came around me a company of the Haw Fields, commanded by Captain Lerbe, which plainly and evidently appeared to me that there was but treachery meant. On Sunday, the 10th. of February, I fell in the rear of Captain Gholson and Captain Hines, and following their trail, came on them at dusk, and after some firing that night, we rode off, and came on them next morning, and we came upon terms of peace, till I could write to their superior, for which I have counselled with some of my officers, and we joined hand and heart, to comply with the terms underneath written.

"We, the subscribers, do acknowledge ourselves subjects to the British Government, and as you are well assured of our fidelity and loyalty to his majesty, and has been daily the case that we have been destroying one another's persons and property to uphold our opinions, and we are hereby willing to come to a cessation of arms for three months, on the condition underwritten.

Our request is, from Cumberland, twenty miles north, and thirty miles east and west, to be clear of any of your light horse. And further, that every man that has been in actual arms, in a permanent order, in order to establish a Royal Government excepting those that have deserted from a regular troop, who have voluntarily enlisted themselves, them we do obligate to deliver up, and each and every man that is at liberty, shall have a right to withdraw in the said district, and that any persons living in the said district that have been in actual arms in a permanent manner to establish the Royal Government, that we should at any request by writing to me or Major Reins, have them apprehended and sent to any of the American officers at or near the line.

That, if any of our men should go out of the line or district, to plunder or distress or murder any of the American party, that we will, by information made to me or Major Reins, or any of the Captains, that I shall return their names. If their request is granted, that they shall immediately be apprehended and sent to you or the next officer, to be tried by your own law: and if any of your party shall be caught plundering, stealing or murdering, or going private paths with arms, signifying as it they were for mischief, to be left to our pleasure, to deal with as we see cause agreeable to our laws. All public roads to be free, by any army or company keeping the public roads, or wagons.

That every person that has been in actual arms in a permanent manner in order to establish the Royal Government, shall not be interrupted of his arms or provisions, and any person that has not been in arms as above mentioned. If you should want provisions or any other articles from them, to send to either of us, and we will send a sufficient guard to see them safe in and out, the Quakers excepted, and that we will not in the mean time distress or disturb any person abiding by your law on the said district in their persons or property.

All back plunder shall be void, as it is impossible to replace or restore all the plunder on either side.

Our request is to have a free trade to any part, with wagons or horse back, with a pass from any appointed officer for salt or iron, or any other necessary, and we expect the two Coxe's Mills to be free from all armies belonging to America.

Any man that has, been returned a Continental, without taking the county, that has been in actual arms as above written, shall return in the said District

If the request is granted above written, I should request the liberty to send to Charleston to let them know what we are about, and any request you should ask in reason, I will petition for, and perhaps a peace might be made for a twelve month, or more' if you desire it.

If the request can't be granted, be pleased to let me know as quick as possible, and if you don't like to comply with our terms, send me an answer back immediately, that we may know what to depend on. So, no more at present, but we remain friends, in behalf of his Majesty's Troops.

Sir, we remain your faithful and humble servants,
DAVID FANNING, Colonel,
JOHN REINS, Major,
WILLIAM REINS, Captain,
JOHN EAGLE, Captain,
WILLIAM PRICE, Captain,
JACOB MANER, Ensign.

We would not blame Fanning, nor any other man, when honestly holding an office under the Royal Government, for standing firm in his place, and performing with all fidelity the duties of the trust reposed in him, provided he does it according to the rules of civilized and Christian warfare; but we would blame any one, Whig or Tory, for violating all the principles of honor and humanity, and for employing all his energies and resources, merely to gratify the low spirit of malice and revenge.

Supposing that it might be gratifying to many of my readers to see something of the judicial proceedings, and of the summary manner in which justice was administered during those troublous times, I have extracted from the records of the circuit court in Hillsboro' the account of the sentence passed upon the three of Fanning's men, mentioned above, and and one or two others.

At a Court of Sessions of the Peace, Oyer and Terminer, General Gaol delivery begun and held for the district of Hillsboro' at Hillsboro' on Thursday the Seventeenth Day of January, Anno Dom, 1782, pursuant to a commission issued by the Governor for the time being; bearing date the 19th day of December, 1781, which commission for holding said Court was read, &c.

Present the Honorable John Williams, Esquire.

SENTENCE,

Saturday, January 26th, 1782.

"The Court met according to adjournment, Present the Honorable JOHN WILLIAMS, Esquire.

Samuel Poe, Indicted and Convicted of Burglary.
Thomas Rickets, Indicted and Convicted of High Treason.
Meredith Edwards, Indicted and Convicted of High Treason.
Thomas Estridge. Indicted and Convicted of High Treason.
Thomas Dark, Indicted and Convicted of High Treason.
William Duke, and Thomas Hunt, } Indicted and Convicted of Horse Stealing.

Being brought into Court and to the Bar, received the following sentence, That you the said Samuel Poe, Thomas Rickets, Meredith Edwards, Thomas Estridge, Thomas Dark, William Duke and Thomas Hunt, and each of you, be taken from thence to the place whence you came, and from thence to the place of execution, and there be hung by the neck and each of your necks until you are dead.

Ordered that the Sheriff of the County of Orange, or for want of such officer, the Coroner of the said county, carry into execution the above sentence of the Court, in the following manner, that is to say, the sentence against Samuel Poe, Thomas Rickets and Thomas Dark, on Friday the first day of February next, between the hours of Eleven o'clock in the forenoon, and two o'clock in the afternoon.

And the sentence of Meredith Edwards, Thomas Estridge, William Duke and Thomas Hunt, be carried into execution on the first day of March next, between the hours of eleven o'clock in the forenoon and two o'clock in the afternoon.

It being recommended to the Court, that the estate of Thomas Estridge, (who this Term was condemned for high treason,) consisting of the following articles, to wit: pork of hogs, eight cows and one mare, seized and in possession of Colonel Benjamin Seawell, of Franklin county; also a small quantity of house hold furniture.

Ordered by the Court, that the above articles be assigned to the wife of the said Thomas Estridge, for the maintenance of said wife and family; and that a copy of this order be transmitted to the said Colonel Seawell, or Commissioner of confiscated property, of said county of Franklin.

Ordered that the following articles of the estate of Thomas Dark, (who this term was condemned for high Treason,) to wit four head cattle, two horses, one mare, and some household furniture, be assigned to the wife of the said Thomas Dark, for the maintenance of the said wife and family.

Ordered that one cow and bed of the estate of Thomas Rickets, (who in this Court was condemned for high Treason,) be assigned to the wife of the said Thomas Rickets, for the support of said wife and family.

(Teste) A. TATOM,
Clk. Pro. Tem.

The threat in the above communication, which is copied from the University Magazine, seems to have been fulfilled with too much punctuality, and from that time he appears to have become more desperate than ever. Among civilized and Christian nations, especially for the last two or three generations, no class of men make greater pretentions to those feelings of humanity and those generous impulses which prompt them to spare the fallen and to protect the feeble, than the officers of an army; and an officer of rank and character could not bring on himself a greater reproach than by wanton cruelty to a surrendered foe, to the aged and infirm, or to women and children. The sexes, however much they may envy and malign, hate and destroy their own, are generally chary of each other, and the man who, can deliberately take the life of a woman is universally regarded as a maniac or a monster. Probably every man of true courage and manliness, if he must die a violent death, would prefer to be killed by a savage, a lion, or a tiger, a reptile, an insect, or any thing in the world rather than by a woman; for before such an act could be committed, he must have done somthing which was beyond all human endurance, or she must have been by some blighting influence, so divested of all the kind and noble qualities of her nature as to have no longer any moral or social affinity with her race. All men of honorable feelings respect a virtuous woman, especially if she is a wife or a mother; and she must have a fiendish or a swinish nature who can corrupt the pure or revel with the vile; but Fanning had no such refined feelings and no such sense of honor. Though a British Colonel and in correspondence with British officers of high standing, neither promotion in the service of the King, nor converse with men of better principles, could revolutionize his moral nature nor bring him under the habitual control of more generous and lofty sentiments.

During this period, though a married man, he succeeded in seducing the wife of a Whig, in the absence of her husband, and, after keeping her for a short time, he murdered her in cold blood. On meeting her at their place of assignation, which was in the woods and not very far from the house, he pretended to be jealous of her and charged her with the want of fidelity. She denied in the most solemn manner, that there was any foundation for the charge, and declared that since she had taken up with him she had not thought of any other; but it was of no avail. He had accomplished his purpose and wanted to get clear of her. He pulled out his pistol, therefore, and shot her dead on the spot, when on her knees and begging for her life. I got this incident from a gentleman of much intelligence in that region, who has felt great interest in gathering up the incidents of the Revolutionary war; and he told me that, horrid as it was, there was no doubt of the fact.

An act of such perfidy, baseness and cruelty, caused a coldness ever after, between Fanning and his brother in-law, William Kerr, whose sister he had married; and although some correspondence was kept up between them occasionally, while they both lived, it was neither frequent nor cordial. Kerr is reported to have been a man of more humanity and more honorable feelings than almost any other in the corps; and he resented it, not only for the immorality of the act, and on his sister's account but for the atrocity of the deed. He soon after left the service, and there never was any harmonious or friendly intercourse between them afterwards. It is said that Fanning made other attempts ot the kind; but so far as any reliable accounts are known, this was the only case in which he succeeded. When we think of those times with all their perils and sufferings thus spread out before us, with the reports of their atrocities and abominations still ringing in our ears, with the light of Christianity shining around us in so much purity and brightness, and with all the blessings of peace and tranquility, freedom and civilization, flowing in upon us from every side, and in such increasing exuberance, we are made to feel that we need no friendly monitor to keep us in mind of our obligations, and no homily to make us pray with all the fervor of which we are capable, that such times may never return.

The two following incidents are copied from the University Magazine, "William Lindley was one of Fanning's favorite friends and one of his captains. He was a respectable man and beloved by his neighbors, and took no part in Fanning's cruelties. Towards the close of the war, when the Tories began to think that the cause of Independence would eventually triumph, Lindley, with many other of the Tories, thought it prudent to leave the part of the country where they were known and retire to distant parts. Lindley crossed the Blue Ridge and determined to remain on New river until the fate of the war was determined. During his command under Fanning, he had given some offence to William White and John Magaharty, two of the Tories belonging to Fanning's party. They pursued Lindley and killed him.

Upon their return, Fanning, having heard of the murder of his friend, resolved to hang them as soon as he could apprehend them. In a little time White and Magaharty fell into his hands, and he hanged them together on the same limb."

"White's wife was pregnant. He gave her a particular account of the murder of Lindley, describing the wounds on his head and the loss of the fingers of one of his hands, which were cut off by the sword in his attempt to save his head from the blow. The story made such an impression upon White's wife, that her child, when born, exhibited a remarkable appearance, had marks on its head, and the fingers of one hand were declared by the mother to be precisely such as White had described to her to have been those of Lindley."

For the following letter I am indebted to Gov. Swain; and give it to the reader as illustrative of the state of things then existing in the country. It was addressed to General Butler by Col. O'Neal, a man who, according to the testimony of his neighbors, loved to keep up appearances, but never fought in one battle, nor exposed himself to the fire of an enemy, and never did anything in the cause of Independence, except to receive pay for nominal services and take advantage of his office as Colonel to extort upon the people of his district. Such men are to be found everywhere and in the most trying times, men who have neither courage, nor patriotism, nor generosity, and who are so cowardly or so avaricious as to be intent on their gains even when their countrymen around them are suffering and struggling for freedom. If Colonel O'Neal, with the men who were under his command and whom he could, at any time, summon to his standard, had been out bravely opposing that notorious freebooter, Col. Fanning he would have done better service to his country than by writing such a puff at his fireside; but a man of this description may tell the truth, especially when telling it may help to keep him in countenance; and therefore we submit this letter to the reader's perusal.

To GENERAL BUTLER.

MARCH 1st, 1782.

Dear Sir,

I had an opportunity of seeing Doctor Boyd yesterday. He informs me that he saw Captain Hanly who informed him that he was in action with Fanning, twelve surprised eighteen, killed six and took three prisoners and a negro, the Conjuror.

Lieutenant Davie who had a very fine mare was appointed to take Fanning in case he ran. Fanning got about forty yards the start of him, but came within four rods in riding five miles. After the mare failed and Fanning cleared himself, but I expect he is taken now.

I hope, Sir, that if there is any new particulars, in your letter you will let me know as I am very fond of good news.

I am Sir,
your friend and humble serv't.
WM. O'NEAL.

As an evidence of the strong and universal detestation in which his character and conduct were held, he was excepted in every treaty and every enactment that was made in favor of the royalists. "Sabine, in his lives of the loyalists, states that when General Marion came to terms with Major Gainey, and conceded to him the privileges of the "neutral ground", Fanning was expressly excepted from the arrangement. He was one of only three persons excluded by name from all benefits under the general "Act of Pardon and Oblivion" of offences committed during the Revolution. [Passed in 1783, Chapter VI. Section 3.]

While his confederates, Colonels Hector McNeill and Duncan Ray, though their operations, when acting separately, were confined to the intermediate region between the Cape Fear and Peedee rivers, when pressed, they found safe refuge in the Raft Swamp, the neighboring morasses, and occasionally in the "neutral ground" in South Carolina, which the necessities of his position compelled General Marion, to accord to Major Gainey when he surrendered," but Fanning was expressly excluded from this privilege, and his operations were confined, for the most part, to the upper country.

On the same day they overtook a young man by the name of Daniel Clifton, who had been on a visit to some of his relations, who lived on the Peedee, and was returning to his home in Virginia. They took him as a prisoner; and passing by the same tree on which Fanning had hanged White and Magaherty, they halted for a few minutes, and hanged Clifton on the same limb."

About the time the foregoing letter was written, and for some weeks after, a state of suffering and distress existed in Randolph county, especially in the upper parts of it, which can be hardly conceived. Many of the most respectable men in the country, prominent Whigs, who had been active in the cause, and a number of peaceable, inoffensive men, who had taken no active part on either side, were murdered in the most shocking manner. Houses and barns were burned with everything they contained. Provisions, bedding and comforts of every kind were destroyed; and many families hitherto in affluent circumstances, were left to beggary or absolute starvation. All this was done from an insatiable spirit of revenge, and not from any hope of maintaining his ground, or of materially aiding the British cause; for at this time, the spring of 1782, the British had been driven from the country; the great mass of the Tories had been completely subdued, and all hope of success had vanished. The reader will now recollect Fanning's letter to Governor Burke, in which he made the bold independant threat, that if the execution of his men who had been apprehended, and were then under sentence of death, was not stopped, he would retaliate "ten fold for one", and that "no officer or private of the rebel party," who might fall into his hands hereafter, should escape instant death. Knowing the spiteful, reckless and daring character of Fanning, the Governor ought, at once to have sent a detachment into that region,, sufficient to capture him forthwith, or drive him out of the country; but probably he had it not in his power, or did not apprehend that, as his number of men was now considerably reduced, he would be able to fulfil his threats. It would not, however, be difficult, even at this late day, to show that he did literally, if not more than literally, fulfil it; and it is said that some monuments of his atrocities may yet be seen. He made only one excursion into the north-west portion of Randolph county; but that was one of Saracen fury and most terrible destruction. For a fuller account of this excursion than I had previously obtained, I am indebted to George C. Mendenhall, Esquire, who at my request, very promptly and kindly undertook to obtain all the facts he could from Isaac Farlow, a respectable member of the Quaker society, who is now an old man, in the eighty-seventh year of his age, but seems to retain all his faculties unimpaired. He lives on Deep river, just in the neighborhood where many of these atrocities were committed, and well recollects all that he saw or heard. From his statements I have been able to trace the sequence of events better than in any previous accounts that I had received; and he gives some additional facts of considerable interest. To converse with such a man is like being carried back to those days, and set down amidst the very scenes of desolation and wretchedness, as they actually existed.

The first victim of his revenge, or the first one of any note, was Colonel Andrew Balfour, who lived in the south west part of Randolph county, and about ten miles from Ashboro'. Only two years before he had represented the county in the Legislature, and was much esteemed in the neighborhood. He was a man of intelligence and public spirit, highly patriotic, liberal in his views and of an irreproachable character. He was at the time just recovering from an attack of sickness, and was unable either to fight or make his escape; but when he had his passions excited or was burning with revenge, Fanning knew no pity. His enemy was in his power and that was enough. He had before plundered Balfour's house, in his absence, and had now come to take his life, which he did in the most barbarous and shocking manner, in the presence of his sister and little daughter, eight or nine years of age, who were both trampled upon and treated with savage barbarity. This was on Sunday, March 10th, 1782, and was, certainly one of the most base and cruel deeds of his bloody career. Some of the descendants of that little daughter are now among our most estimable and useful citizens; but we will give a fuller account of Colonel Balfour and of his tragical end, in a separate article.

From this scene of cruelty and bloodshed they went to the house of William Milliken, Esq., who lived on Back creek, about two miles south of Johnsonville or the old cross roads. As Milliken was not at home they burned all his buildings, and destroyed every thing they could. On going to a house, if he got the man and took his life, he never burned the house nor destroyed any other property, except perhaps to take just what grain or provisions they needed at the time; but if he failed to get the man, he then destroyed everything he could and seemed to delight in causing as much distress to the family as possible. While Milliken's house was on fire, as Farlow states, his wife Jane, carried out a favorite feather bed; but they carried it back and threw it on the fire. When the bed began to burn, they twisted a stick into the feathers and scattered them over the house. When the blazing feathers as they flew in every direction through the rooms, caught in a large bundle of yarn, which being on the wall, they only taunted Mrs. Milliken, and said, "Look at your yarn, old woman." On leaving Milliken's, they compelled his son Benjamin and a young man by the name of Joshua Lowe to go along and pilot them to the house of Col. John Collins, where he met with a disappointment; for Collins was not at home, but they burned his house.

He next went to the house of Colonel John Collier, who was the Senator for Randolph county, and in other respects a prominent man. He had been appointed County Surveyor, but either being unacquainted with the business himself, or not having time for it, he had brought a young man, by the name of William Clarke, from Virginia, to do the surveying. Clarke soon found where the vacant lands lay and entered them. Frequently he entered lands on which people were living, but whether with good title deeds or not I have not learned; but this seems to have been done chiefly with those who were regarded as Tories, or who were not on the Whig side, and perhaps with such as he thought could be frightened into measures. After awhile he employed Ralph Lowe, and a man by the name of Linden, to sell these lands for him. "Nathan Farlow" says my informant, "had to pay a fat steer and some gold for his land;" but in process of time, Nathan Farlow owned all the lands of these men and he himself. Isaac Farlow, now lives on the Lowe land. It was believed by the sufferers that these things were done by Collier's connivance, if not by his express direction; and while his prominence as a Whig made him a special object of Fanning's vengeance, he had incured, justly or unjustly, the ill will of all that class in the neighborhood, and probably in the whole or a large part of the county.

On the night of Fanning's attack, he was at home, and asleep; but being well aware that he ran a considerable risk in doing so, before he lay down he placed a young man by the name of Benjamin Fincher, as sentinel, on a pile of rails, at the distance of a few rods from the house, and left his horse tied near the door, where he had fed him in a hominy mortar, probably with the saddle on and ready to be mounted at a moment's warning. As the assailants approached, and Fincher hailed them, Fanning made his two Whig pilots, Miliken and Lowe, answer that they were friends. Becoming more and more uneasy as they approached so mysteriously, he kept hailing them, and they kept answering that they were friends until they got pretty near, when two guns were fired at him; but having on a strong, tight vest, the balls glanced and did him no serious injury. My informant, Isaac Farlow, saw Fincher the next day, and the marks of the bullets on the vest. When they fired on Fincher, he hopped off the rail pile, and ran for life, leaving his musket behind him. The firing roused Colonel Collier, and springing instantly to his feet, cried out, "Parade! parade! boys, parade!" Such a command, uttered with so much boldness, and by a man of his standing and influence, made Fanning pause for a moment, and this allowed Collier time to mount his horse and escape; but the house was burned and the premises made a scene of utter desolation. He lived about three miles from Bell's mill, and in a south-west direction. He went the same night to the house of Captain John Bryant, who lived about half a mile from New Market, and on the place now owned and occupied by Joseph Newland; but missed his way and went to the house of Stephen Harlin, who was a Quaker, if I mistake not, or at least an inoffensive kind of a man. Fanning did not molest him; but compelled two of his daughters, Betsy and Elsy, to go along and show him the way to Bryant's house. On riding up they first enquired for the man of the house, and were told that he was tending Walker's mill, on Sandy creek, when one of them exclaimed with an oath, "Here is Walker, now." They then began enquiring who lived in this direction and who lived in that direction, until Bryant was named, when they said that was the place to which they wished to go, and made these two daughters of Walker's miller get up behind and go along as pilots. When they came up they made a rush against the door to burst it open, but it was fast barred. The noise waked Bryant, however, and he asked "Who is there?" They answered, Colonel Fanning, and asked him to open the door. He told them to wait till he got his breeches on; but they damned him and his breeches too. He, Bryant, called a young man who was in the house, to get up, but he thought it was all a jest when they told him that Fanning was there. They called upon him to surrender; and when he asked them what they would do with him if he did surrender, they answered that they would *parole* him, but he replied, "Damn you and your parole too. I have had one, and I will never take another." Fanning then spoke, and said, "My life for his, if Walker don't kill him." The Miss Harlins, whom they had brought along as pilots, entreated him to surrender, assuring him that Fanning was there; but not it, he cursed Fanning and the whole of them. He opened the door a little way to admit the girls, and one of them started to go in; but Walker caught her by the dress and pulled her back, swearing that she was going in to protect Bryant. Bryant seems to have been a brave but reckless kind of a man. After holding out as long as he could, he opened the door, and going out on the step, said, "Gentlemen, I surrender;" but instantly he was shot down, and fell back against his wife, who was standing just behind him. As she was raising him up, another of the company stepped forward and shot him in the eye. Fanning then threatened death to any one who should give the alarm before daylight; but, according to his custom, as he had killed the man he was after, he destroyed no property and did no further damage. As he probably felt a little wearied after so many labors, he lay down in the cradle, and after rocking himself there very comfortably for some time, while the rest were sauntering about, they all gathered up and went off in quest of other victims.

As soon as they were gone, Richard Isaacs, who lived at Bryants, went over to Farlow's and told them what had been done. He and his wife, Ruth, went over to Bryant's before daylight; but Nathan stopped at some distance from the house until he ascertained whether he could go with safety. His wife on entering the house, found the dead body of Bryant lying on the door sill, with the head inside and the legs and feet outside. What had become of Mrs. Bryant and the children, in the meantime,—whether they had been driven away or frightened away by the ruffians, or finding that they could do nothing with it, after Isaacs left, they were letting it lie until some of the neighbors would come in, and were giving vent to their grief, I have not learned; —but, by daylight, Nathan Farlow and his wife had the corpse *laid out*. At sunrise, Isaac Farlow, my informant, went over himself, and saw the body and the two bullet holes. The first ball had entered his breast and the other his head; but neither of them had passed through him. Bryant was a daring, fearless kind of a man. An old friend in that neighborhood told me that he could have made his escape from the back door, if he had done it as soon as the alarm was given; but that he scorned to run from his enemies, and did not surrender until he found they were about setting fire to the house. When he cursed them and their parole too, they told him in language which would then have been understood any where, that they would "parole him the *near way to Georgia*," and, going to some "log heaps" which were burning in a field, not far from the house, they got a "chunk" or brand for the purpose of burning the house, with all that it contained. Seeing that they were determined on his death, and rather than let his wife and children be burned up in the house with him, he opened the door, went out on the step and offered to surrender, but was instantly shot down.

After Fanning and his troop had left Bryant's something like an hour, they returned and enquired the way to Colonel Dougan's house. They burned his house with all the buildings on the premises, and destroyed everything they could. After leaving Dougan's, and in the course of the same day, they captured a Whig and hung him on the spot. The Whigs had, some time before, hung a Tory, by the name of Isaac Jackson, on the limb of a tree which stood by a shoft turn in the road near Brower's and Spinks'; and Fanning had sworn that he would hang five Whigs on the same limb for every Tory the Whigs hung; but, old Friend Farlow says they mistook the limb and hung him on a limb close by the one on which the Tory had been hanged; for he knew both the limbs. They cut a notch on the limb on which they hung the Whig, using it as a talley, and intending to cut an additional notch for every Whig they hung on it until their number was complete; but fortunately for the country, he was disappointed for this proved to be his first and last visit into that neighborhood.

During this expedition up Deep river, which included some three or four days, a little incident occurred which, though of small importance in itself, was rather amusing than otherwise, and showed the terror of his name, of which old Friend Farlow gives the following account.

A troop of Light-horse, from the foot of the Blue

Ridge, or what was then called the Hollows, in Surry county, came down Deep river into the Coxes' settlement, on the hunt of Fanning, and after giving him a chase, as they said, in the morning, but without success, they loaded themselves with plunder from the settlers of the neighborhood, such as knives and forks, plates, spoons, &c. Having done so, they set off on their return, Isaac Farlow says, and came as far as his uncle George Farlow's, who was then living in a cabin on the road-side, with a small lot enclosed around it. The house stood on the east bank of Web's creek, about three or four miles east from the present town of Ashboro', and is now owned by Joseph Cannon. When the party came opposite to the house, Farlow was standing in the door, and one of the men presented his gun as if about to shoot, but another stopped him and told him not to shoot, for that was the man of the house. Here they halted, sitting on their horses, and gave an account of their adventure in the morning, stating that they had been in pursuit of Fanning that they had given him a hard chase, but without success, and that they were making great boast of what they would do if they could only get a chance at him, when one of them happened to turn his eye down the road and exclaimed, with an oath, "Yonder is Fanning now." Instantly they dashed off, down the hill, which was very steep, and into the creek, all huddled up together. Farlow said there was such a blaze of fire from the guns of Fanning's men, as they passed the door that he thought the others must have been all killed; but not much execution was done. When the mountain party got out of the creek, they left the road and took into the woods, towards the place where Ashboro' now stands, and Fanning's party in hot pursuit. It was neck or nought, and they fled for life, throwing away every incumbrance and strewing their plunder, knives and forks, plates, spoons, and everything else, all through the woods. In a short time Fanning returned, bringing a prisoner with him, who was badly wounded, and stating that they had killed one man in the woods, over the creek; but, on search being made by the neighbors he was not found. Fanning left the wounded man in the care of Farlow, and told him, rather sarcastically, that when he got well, he would be on the hunt of him again; but the wounded man very humbly protested that he never would. Fanning then returned and in the direction from which he came while in pursuit of the mountaineers, and before he had overtaken them, he met stephen Mendenhall and his wife; riding two very good horses, and, as some of his horses were failing, he made them exchange, but told them to stay there until he returned. They did so; and, on his return, he gave them back their own horses.

A troop of Whigs was instantly raised, headed by John Clarke, and went in pursuit. Clarke was a man of as much daring courage and energy of character as Fanning himself, but had not as much stratagem nor adroitness in the execution of his plans. Captain John Gillespie, having probably been sent for, came down with his company from Guilford and joined them. Gillespie feared no man and would have gloried in meeting this enemy of his country. Fanning and his corps had not left the place of execution more than a few minutes when this troop of Whigs, under the command or leadership of John Clarke, came in sight A few of Fanning's men it seems had delayed a little, and having cut down the corpse, were doing something about it, either by way of preparation for burying it, or more probably, they were robbing it, of whatever money, clothes or anything else which the man had about him that was worth carrying away. While thus employed the Whigs came in sight, and they fled. There was a hot pursuit; but the Tories, having the fleetest horses, all made their escape except one who was overtaken by John Dugan, and John Clarke. Dugan's gun or pistol snapped, but Clarke shot and probably inflicted a slight wound. The Tory fell to the ground and lay there and made pretence that he was just breathing his last. Being deceived by appearances and wishing to overtake the rest if possible, they left him, as they supposed, in his last agonies; but as soon as they were out of sight, he jumped up and rejoicing at the success of his stratagem, ran for dear life.

From this time until he left the State, I have been able to get no consistent or satisfactory account; but it was probably soon after the transactions above related, that he was so befooled by James Harding; for his right-hand man, the bloody Walker, was killed or mortally wounded on that occasion; but he was with Fanning on this bloody excursion up the river. It is known however that he continued his murders and depredations for some weeks, probably two months longer and with a virulence increasing in proportion as his fortunes became desperate. Many of his men left him and went to the mountains or other places where they would be beyond the reach of law and the vengeance of the other party; but a number adhered to him until the last, with a firmness and a zeal worthy of a better cause. We presume that it was on their return from their murderous and devastating excursion up Deep river that they went to Bell's mill and made an attack upon his house in the night; but were frightened away by a well-managed stratagem of Mrs. Bell, a fuller account of which will be given in a separate sketch of her character, sufferings and patriotic services during the war.

CAPTURE OF ANDREW HUNTER.

Everybody in the whole country has, probably, heard something about the capture of Andrew Hunter by Fanning; and of his singular and almost miraculous escape. The incident was one of the last in Fanning's career; and the account of it here given, is taken in part from Judge Murphy's papers as published in the University Magazine and partly from other sources.

It seems that Hunter was a Whig, and lived on the waters of Little river, in the south or south-west part of Randolph county. In addition to the well known fact that he was a Whig, and a decided advocate of independence, he had made some remarks about Fanning, which having come to his ears, had so excited his wrath, that he had sworn to take Hunter's life, if he ever got him in his power. When Hunter and John Latham, one of his neighbors, were going with a cart to market, on Pedee, for the purpose of getting salt and some other necessaries for their families, they saw Fanning and his corps approaching. Latham was walking beside the horse, and Hunter was riding in the cart. He was well aware of Fanning's purpose to take his life and he knew that it would be perfectly useless for him to think of escaping on foot through the open pine woods. As the only thing in his power, he covered himself up as well as he could in the cart, and left the rest to an all-wise Providence. When Fanning came up he stopped the cart, and asked Latham where he was going. He said he was going to such a place on the Pedee to get salt and some other necessaries. "What have you in your cart?" Some flaxseed, beeswax &c." "Have you any thing to eat?" Latham told him that he had a little, but he hoped they would not take it from him, as it was very difficult to get any thing on that road. Fanning swore he didn't care for that; and, as they were hungry, they would have it. He then dismounted and entered the front end of the cart to search for provision; but, at the first haul, he uncovered Hunter, and exclaimed, with a kind of malignant joy, "Ah you internal rascal—I have got you now. Come out here, and be saying your prayers as fast as you can; for you have very few minutes to live." Hunter obeyed of course; and Fanning, in a minute or two brought out the provisions.

It was Fanning's design to dispose of Hunter at once and was giving his orders to that effect; but some of his men remarked to him that, as they were very hungry, they had better eat first, and let "the poor devil" have a little time to prepare for death. To this proposal, Fanning and the rest agreed; and, throwing the rope with which he was to be hung, at his feet, they told him that he had only fifteen minutes to live. Then they all stacked their arms against a large tree, close by, and set their grinders to work in good earnest, taking care to keep Hunter between them and the cart. In this situation, while trying to pray, he was trying to watch, and at the same time, he prepared to act if occasion should offer. The first thought that came into his mind, was to seize a gun, and sell his life as dearly as he could; but the same thought started up in Fanning's mind at the same moment; and he said to his men, "Stand by your guns, or that rascal will get one and kill some of us before we know what we are about." He next thought of the "Bay Doe," and a swelling emotion of hope arose in his bosom, that if he could only get on her back, there might be some probability of his escape; but even a look that way, would reveal his intentions, and quench the last ray of hope.

Before the fifteen minutes were expired, one of the men by the name of Small, rose up with his gun in his hand; and Hunter begged that he would intercede with Fanning to spare his life. As they conversed together they, unconsciously perhaps to themselves, advanced a few feet, and this brought them close to the Bay Doe, where she was standing with her bridle loosely thrown on a bush. Upon Small's telling him that there was no hope for him, he leaped forward, vaulted into Fanning's saddle, and throwing himself forward, lay as flat on her shoulders as he could. With his left hand, he disengaged or took up the bridle; but the mare unwilling, perhaps to leave the other horses, did not start at once. Orders were instantly given to shoot him; and Small, though at the distance of a few paces, fired at him without effect. The firing of the gun started the mare at full speed; and she being Fanning's favorite nag, he was about as anxious for her safety as he was for the death of the rider. Hunter said afterwards that as he darted off, he heard Fanning telling them to kill the rascal, but take care and not kill his mare. As he lay so close to the mare's withers, it required a very good marksman, or very good luck, to miss her and hit the rider, and three more guns were fired at him, but he was still unhurt. He heard the bullets whistling by him on every side; but his only chance was to keep his position and go ahead.

A fifth shot lodged a ball in the fleshy part of his shoulder, which disabled his arm, but so intense was the excitement of his mind, that he was hardly aware of the injury. William Kerr, Fanning's brother in law, was the one who shot him; but this was not generally known until some time after. He pressed forward and was closely pursued for a mile, but when they lost sight of him he began to breathe more freely, and he saw the blood running down the mare's shoulder. The first thought which passed through his mind, was that the mare must be badly wounded, and if so, his case might still be a hopeless one. After a moment's examination, he ascertained that the wound was not in the mare but in himself. A slug had lodged in the lower part of the shoulder and his arm was nearly or quite powerless. He kept the road for two or three miles, when he turned into the woods and rode ten miles further to the house of Nathaniel Steed, bleeding profusely all the way. As soon as he alighted he fainted; and Steed collected a party of men to guard him. He also sent for a physician who dressed his wound, and in a few days he was sent to Salisbury, where the ball was extracted, and he got well.

In the hurry of pursuit, Fanning had neglected to notice, or to trace the blood which marked the route of Hunter, and continued up the road to Hunter's house. Finding that Hunter had escaped, and that his mare, with the brace of pistols presented to him by Major Craig, at Wilmington, were lost, he determined to wreak his vengeance on Hunter's family. After plundering the house, he took Mrs. Hunter, then far advanced in pregnancy, and all of Hunter's negroes, and conducted them to a lonely place in the woods in the county of Moore, on Bear creek. From this place he despatched a messenger to Hunter with an offer to return his wife and negroes if Hunter would send back his mare and pistols. Hunter returned for answer, that the mare had been sent away and he could not get her. This answer was delivered to Fanning in the evening of the 5th day after he had taken up camp in the woods in Moore. The sun was about half an hour high when the answer was returned, and Fanning immediately mounted and went off, taking with him Hunter's negroes and leaving Mrs. Hunter alone. Smally, after proceeding a short distance, returned to Mrs. Hunter and informed her where she would find a path near the camp which led to a house not far distant. Mrs. Hunter proceeded to the house, where she was kindly treated, and from which she was sent home. It is probable, from this conduct of Smally, that Hunter's entreaties at the cart had weighed upon his feelings, and that when he fired on Hunter, he intentionally missed him. "Hunter was still living when Judge Murphy collected his information, and had long resided in South Carolina, on the Pedee river, above Mars' Bluff. He was a man of respectability and wealth, and his adventure with Fanning had not then ceased to be an interesting topic of conversation to his friends."

That the blood of the Bay Doe has been well known and highly appreciated ever since, is proved from the following facts.

Some forty years ago, more or less, Colonel M——, a gentleman in one of the neighboring counties, who took much delight in the amusements of the turf, and who attained a great deal of celebrity among the sporting gentry of the State, had a mare which, from her blood, he called the Bay Doe, and which never was beat, except when she flew the track, a thing which she was very apt to do. On one occasion, when heavy bets were pending, she flew the track; and in her reckless flight, bounded like a deer over a very high fence, which caused her to fall, and crippled her so badly that it was supposed she never could be run again. An important race was soon after to take place in Salisbury, which Colonel M——, as a matter of course, attended, and took her with him; but, as she was still a little lame, he had no thought of putting her on the track. A friend, or an intimate acquaintance of his, a gentleman who lived in an adjoining county, by unfortunate bets of the kind, or in some other way, had so far reduced his property that he thought it necessary to remove with his family to the far west, and was in Salisbury on his way to the west when the races came on. Without consultation or enquiry, he at once bet five hundred dollars on the Bay Doe; and when he told Colonel M—— what he had done, he replied that he was very sorry to hear it; for, as the mare was not yet entirely recovered from her lameness, she could not be run, and he would lose his money. However; they concluded, about midnight or after, when every body else was asleep, that they would go out with her, nearly a mile and a half from town, and take her round the path to see whether it would be at all worth while to enter her for the next day's race ; but she flew the track again, threw the rider and dashed back, or rather flew back to town as if all the witches in creation had been after her. From this exhibition of her recruited strength and agility, Colonel M—— concluded that he would give his friend a chance, at all events, and put her on the track. Contrary to all expectation, she behaved very genteely, indeed, and "swept stakes." This lucky bet so far relieved the gentleman from his embarrassments that he at once gave out his removal to the west, and returned with his family, to their former neighborhood.

Not more than two or three years ago, a suit was decided in Randolph Court, Judge Battle on the bench, which depended on proving the stock of the Bay Doe, and shows that her blood is to this day well known and highly valued in the county. It is a wonder that horses have not been advertised under the name of the Red Buck, and tracing their pedigree back to Fanning's stock, or blooded mares selling for hundreds of dollars because they are descended from Fanning's Bay Doe. People in this country have been giving immense prices for "blooded horses," English horses, when we have horses in this country that have as much blood and as good blood as those which are imported from Europe or any other continent.

The Bay Doe saved Hunter's life on another occasion, and did it by performing a feat, which is well worthy of record; or at least, such is the tradition in the neighborhood, and it probably has some foundation in truth. It is said that when he was riding the Bay Doe, on the high ground, south of Deep river, and not far above the Buffalo ford, where the village of Franklinville now stands, he was like to be overtaken by some of Fanning's men. He first attempted to gain the ford; but found they were heading him in that direction. He then turned his course up the river, but they were there ready to receive him. The only alternative was to surrender, which would be certain and instant death, or to make a desperate plunge down a precipice, some fifty feet high into the river. He chose the latter, and escaped unhurt. The descent is not perpendicular; but makes an angle with the horizon, probably, of sixty degrees. It is also rough and craggy. Any one who will look at it from the road, on the north side of the river, will say that it was a greater feat of horsemanship than that of General Putnam in riding down the stone steps at the church. It was such a daring adventure that his pursuers, though they rode like Tartars, were mounted on the best of horses, and were burning with revenge would not dare to follow him, but stopped short, in a kind of amazement, and contented themselves with firing two or three pistols after him As there was no level ground at the bottom of the descent, he plunged right into the river and turned down the stream, sometimes swimming and sometimes on *terra firma* or floundering over rocks, until he found a place where he got out on the north side and made his escape.

Very few of Fanning's officers died a natural death; and not more than two or three of them, so far as I have learned, ever became citizens of even common respectability. Major John Reins, Jr. was in 1819 living in Tennessee, very poor, and keeping a mill,. Richard Edwards was killed at Kirk's farm the week before the battle of Cane creek. Edward Edwards, his brother, who then took the command, was killed the next week at

Lindley's mill. Meredith Edwards was indicted for treason about the beginning of 1782. John Reins, Sr., was killed at Lindley's mill. John Eagle was shot or hanged near Pedee. James Price was hanged near the same place. David Jackson was hanged by Colonel Lopp near Fork creek in the lower end of Randolph county. Thomas Darke was hanged at Hillsboro' in 1782. John Willison fled to Pennsylvania, and lived very poor. John Lindley, the same. Stephen Walker was shot in April, in 1782, by Colonel Gholson, on Deep river. James Lindley was shot near the mountains; and. as I understood, Simon Lindley, the same. Others say that he was shot in his own neighborhood, under the suspicion that he had murdered his wife. William Lindley—Ignatius Wallaston fled to Pennsylvania, where he was alive long after the war, and was a bricklayer by trade. Thomas Blair removed to the mountains and settled on New river, where he built iron works and became rich. Thomas Rickets and Thomas Eastridge were indicted for treason.

NAOMI WISE,

—OR,—

THE WRONGS OF A BEAUTIFUL GIRL.

A TRUE STORY,

ENACTED IN NORTH CAROLINA 90 YEARS AGO.

———o:0:o———

TO THE READER.

The truth of what the reader will find and the lesson to be deduced from this story, will commend it to the favor of all the good people of Randolph county, and to the reading public generally. It is not fiction, but a reliable narrative of facts, as gathered from the gray-haired fathers and mothers of to-day.

An account of the present beautiful town of NAOMI FALLS is annexed.

The narrative of Naomi Wise is published from the original history, by M. Penny, Randleman, N. C., with the song, as sung in by-gone days when men stood, in this country, heart to heart and hand to hand.

M. PENNY.

OCTOBER, 1888.

NAOMI WISE.

CHAPTER I.

About ninety years ago there lived where New Salem now is, in the northern part of Randolph County, North Carolina, a very open and warm hearted gentleman by the name of William Adams. A few families of nature's noblest quality lived in the vicnity. They were not emphatically rich, but were what our people called *good livers*; they were honest,, hospitable and kind; they knew neither the luxuries nor the vices of high life. Their farms supplied enough for their own tables, and surplus sufficient for a brisk trade with Fayetteville The wild forest hills and immense glades in the neighborhood, afforded bountiful quantities of game; whilst Deep River abounded with the finest fish. At that time the inhabitants were by no means so thickly settled as at present; *trading* as a regular business was unknown, except to a few merchants. The people were somewhat rude, still, however, hospitable and kind.

At William Adam's lived Naomi Wise. She had early been thrown upon the cold charity of the world, and she had received the frozen crumbs of that charity. Her size was medium; her figure beautifully formed; her face handsome and expressive; her eye keen yet mild; her words soft and winning. She was left without father to protect, mother to counsel, brothers and sisters to love, or friends with whom to associate. Food, clothing and shelter must be earned by the labor of her own hands, not such labor, however, as females at this day perform. There was no place for her but the kitchen with the prospect of occasionally going into the field. This the poor orphan accepted willingly; she was willing to labor, she was ashamed to beg. The thousand comforts that parents can find for their children are never enjoyed by the fatherless. Fanaticism may rave over the chains of the African; the pity of sixtween States can be pour ut for the southern negro' the great meetings are h to move on emancipation; but who pities the *orphan?* May the Lord pity him, for man will not.

At the time of which we speak, neighborhoods were nearly distinct; all that lived in the same vicinity, generally bearing the same name. To account for this, we have only to recollect, that most of our settlers migrated from Pennsylvania and Virginia; and that families generally came and settled together. Physical force being frequently necessary for self-defence, such families made a kind of treaty offensive and defensive. Sometimes, however, the most deadly feuds broke out among themselves. Such was the case with the Lewis family, that settled on Sandy Creek. Old David Lewis probably came from Pennsylvania; at least, an old gentleman by name of Buchanan told the writer so; Buchanan was personally acquainted with the Lewises. David had a considerable family of boys, all of whom were noted for their great size and strength. This was in every respect a very peculiar family, peculiar in appearance, in character, and in destiny. The Lewises were tall, broad, muscular and very powerful men. In the manner of fighting very common at that time, viz: to lay aside all clothing but pantaloons, and then try for victory by striking with the fist; scratching, gouging, and biting, a Lewis was not to be vanquished. The family were the lions of the country. This character was eminently pugnacious. Nearly all of them drank to intoxication; aware of power, they insulted whom they listed; they sought occasions of quarrel as a Yankee does gold dust in California. They rode through plantations; killed their neighbors' cattle: took fish from other men's traps; said what they pleased; all more for contention than gain. Though the oppressed had the power, they were afraid to prosecute them: they knew these human hydras had no mercy; they dreaded their retaliating vengeance. For these men would follow their children while at work, and whip them from one side of the field to the other. They would compel them to stand in the yard during cold rainy nights, till the little creatures were frozen beyond the power of speech; and sometimes their wives shared no better fate. A fine colt belonging to Stephen Lewis, once did some trifling mischief, when the owner, enraged, shot it dead upon the instant. Anything, man or beast, that dared to cross them, periled its life. They neither sheltered themselves under the strong arm of law, nor permitted others to do so; they neither gave nor asked mercy. Yet these same men were unfailing friends, when they chose to protect. Their pledge was sure as anything human could be; if they threatened death or torture, those threatened always thought it prudent to retire to the very uttermost part of the earth; if they vowed protection, their protege felt secure. Some of their remote relations are still in this country; they are among our most worthy citizens, but they never tamely submit to insult. Some inquire how such men as the Lewises could ever intermarry with other families; who would unite themselves to such cold hearted creatures?

While such characters are in some respects to be abhorred, yet there is about them that has in all ages been attractive. Ladies are accused, because they fall in love with fops, of wanting common sense, and of loving vanity rather than substance. The accusation is false. Except the love of a Christian for his Lord, the love of a woman is the *purest* and *truest* thing on earth; sweet as the incense of heaven, soft as the air of paradise, and confiding as the lamb; it scorns the little, the vile and the treacherous. The tendrils of woman's affection despise the shrubs of odor and beauty to entwine closely and eternally around high forest trees that are exposed to howling storms and the thunders of Jove. The trees may be *rough* and *crooked*, but then they are *trees*. Find a man a great intellectual power, of iron will, of reckless daring, but of unshaken fidelity; in such you find a master magnet around which women's hearts collect by natural attraction. But how can a pure and good woman love a wicked man! Nonsense, thou puritan! She does not love his wickedness, but his soul. Did not the Saviour love a wicked world, though he died to destroy its wickedness? Then a woman will love a wicked man better than a good one, will she? No, she will love a good man much best, other things being equal. But you make daring deeds of wickedness the exponents of man's greatness. I do no such thing. I make actions that require power, energy, and firmness, test of greatness; that such actions should be tainted with evil, is a blot that mars them in no small degree; but still they are great actions, i. e. the products of powerful minds, there are certain philosophers in the world that would make all great actions cease to be great, when they ceased to be good; they would make their greatness directly as their goodness. These are evidently two different qualities, the one measuring the action per se, the other its moral character. Genuine love is as follows: woman loves the power which is able to support and protect, and if that power be good she will love it the more : man loves the gentle, confiding one that leans upon him with confidence and trusts him with her destiny : if she be good, he will love her the more. This may be grossly misconstrued ; but *fools will not see*, and the wise can see our meaning, it is therefore plain enough.

We will hazard an axiom or two while on this point. No woman will or can really love a man who is intellectually her inferior. No man can love a woman that has not confidence in his fidelity and protection. If a powerful man be true to his wife, she being what she should, she will love him though he stain his hands in blood, and be guilty of the foulest deeds known in the catalogue of crime. But this is an unpardonable digression, let us return.

But few of the Lewises died natural deaths. Stephen Lewis was most unmerciful to his wife. He frequently whipped her with hobblerods, and otherwise abused her beyond endurance. Finally by aid of Richard, a brother of Stephen's she escaped from home and spent several months at an acquaintance's. Richard at length told Stephen that his wife would return if he would promise never more to abuse her. This he promised upon the word of a Lewis. He therefore told him to come to his house on a certain day, and he would find her. At the time appointed Stephen went, found his wife, and took her on his horse to convey her home. On the way, he made her tell the means of her escape and the agents employed. The agent, as we have said, was his brother Richard. Stephen went home ; kindly told his wife that he should henceforth treat her very kindly, but that he intended to shoot the scoundrel, Richard. Loading his gun, he immediately returned to his brother's. Richard happening to observe his approach and conjecturing the object, fled up stairs with his gun. Stephen entered the house and enquired for Richard. Not learning from the family, and supposing him up stairs, he started up, and as his head came in view, Richard shot him, but did not kill him. Stephen was carried home and for a long time was unable even to sit up, still swearing, however, that when he recovered he would shoot Richard. His brother knowing the threat would be executed, went to the house one day, and while Stephen was sitting on the bedside, having his wounds dressed, through a crack of the house Richard shot him through the heart.

It is said that the manner of men's deaths frequently resembles their lives. The fate of the Lewises seems to confirm the fact. They were heartless tyrants while they lived, and as tyrants deserve, they died cruel and bloody deaths.

CHAPTER II.

――――――Like a lovely tyro
She grew to womanhood, and between whiles
Rejected several suiters, just to learn
How to accept a worse one in his turn.

—Bryon.

Naomi Wise was a lovely girl, just blooming in all the attractiveness of nineteen. Though serving as cook and sometimes as out-door hand, she was the light of the family, and was treated better than such persons usually are. She was neatly dressed, rode to church on a fine horse and was the occasion of many youngsters visiting the house of Mr Adams. Among those who frequently found it convenient to call at Mr. Adams' was Jonathan Lewis. His father, Richard Lewis, the same that shot Stephen, lived near Centre meeting-house, on Polecat creek, in Guilford county. Jonathan was clerking for Benjamin Elliott, at Asheboro, in Randolph and in passing from Centre to Asheboro, it was directly in his way to pass through New Salem. Jonathan like the others of the same name, was a large, well built, dignified looking man. He was young, daring and impetuous. If he had lived in Scotland he would have been a worthy companion for Sir William Wallace or Robert Bruce; in England he would have vied with the Black Prince in coolness and bravery; in France he might have stood by the side of McDonald, in the central charge at Wagram; in our own revolution his bravery and power would, perhaps, have saved the day at Brandywine. He was composed of the fiercest elements; his wrath was like whirlwinds and scathing lightning: his smile like sunbeams bursting through a cloud, illumined every countenance upon which it fell. He never indulged in tricks or small sport, the ordinary passtimes of youth had no attraction for him. The smallest observation would teach us, that such men are capable of anything; once engaged they are champions in the cause of humanity; but once let loose, like unchained lions, they tear to pieces both friends and foes. The greatest men are capable of being the greatest scourges. Leonidas was a rock upon which Persia broke, but some provocation might have made him a rock by which Greece would have been ground to powder. Dirk Hatteraik was a daring smuggler, that in a low, black lugger, defied the power of England; if the government had treated this man wisely, he might have been an admiral to eclipse Nelson. Our daring, headstrong boys are generally given over as worthless; and here is the mistake; the world neither understands the mission nor management of such powerful minds. Bucephalus was pronounced a worthless animal by the whole court of Philip. Alexander alone perceived his value and knew how to manage him; and in fact, Bucephalus was the greatest horse the world ever saw.

Jonathan Lewis saw Naomi Wise and loved her. She was the gentle, confiding, unprotected creature that a man like Lewis, would love by instinct. Henceforward he was a frequent visitor at Adams'. The dark clouds that had so long hovered over the orphan were breaking away; the misty, dim vista of the future opened with clear light and boundless prospects of good; the fogs rolled away from the valley of life, and Naomi saw a pretty pathway bordered with flowers, and crossed only by little rills of purest water. Her young and guileless heart beat with new and higher life; that she was loved by a man so powerful as Lewis, was sufficient recompence for a cheerless childhood. Day and night she labored to procure the indispensables of housekeeping; for in those days it was esteemed disreputable if a girl by the time she was twenty, had not made or earned for herself a bed, some chairs, pots, tubs, &c. And a young lady then modestly displayed her things to her lover, with as much care as modern misses display their painting, needle-work, and acquirements on the piano. Instead of going to the piano, to the dance and other such latter day inventions, youngsters then went with the ladies to milk the cows, and display their gallantry by holding away the calves while the operation was performed; they then accompanied [the damsels to the spring to put away the milk, and brought back a pail of water.

Time flew on, Lewis still continued as clerk, and had

won the good opinion of his employer. Naomi was blooming in all the charms of early womanhood; her love for Lewis was pure and ardent; and the rumor was abroad that a marriage was shortly to take place. But an evil genius crossed the path of Lewis in the shape of his mother. Her ambition and avarice projected for her son a match of different character. She deemed it in the range of possibility that Jonathan might obtain the hand of Hettie Elliott, the sister of Benjamin Elliott, his employer. That mothers are ambitious everybody knows, and that they are the worst of matchmakers is equally well known. But Mrs. Lewis thought Miss Elliott a prize worthy an effort at least. The Elliott were wealthy, honorable and in high repute. They have always stood high in this county, and citizens have delighted to honor them with public favor and private friendship. Mr. B. Elliott, Hettie's brother, evidently prized Lewis highly; he regarded him as an honorable, intelligent and industrious young gentleman, and no doubt thought him a respectable match for his sister. Lewis made some advances to Hettie, which were received in such a way as to inspire hope. This was the turning tide in the fortunes of Lewis. The smile of one superior to Naomi Wise in every respect, except beauty and goodness; the earnest exhortations of an influential mother; and the prospect of considerable property, bore down all obstacles. The pure love to Miss Wise, the native and genuine passion of his own heart, were not equal to a conflict with pride and avarice. Not but that Lewis, as any other man could and would love Miss Elliott. She was accomplished, beautiful, and of charming manners; an Elliott could not be otherwise. But these were not the attractions that won Lewis. Money, family connection, name and station, were the influences that clouded the fair prospects of innocence, opened the flood gates of evil, and involved all the parties concerned in ruin.

Tupper has wisely said that nothing in this world is single, all things are in pairs; and the perfection of earthly existence consists in properly pairing all the separate elements. Two elements properly adapted have a natural attraction, and firmly adhere amid all circumstances of prosperity or disaster; but two elements improperly mated repel each other with natural and undying repulsion in spite of circumstances or calculations. The young instinctively and naturally love those that would make them happy; but pride, family interference and coldhearted calculations often interpose; sordid considerations tear asunder the holiest chords of affection, and vainly attempt to thwart nature's own promptings. Lewis loved Miss Wise for herself; no selfish motive moved his heart or tongue; this would have been a union of peace and joy; he wished to marry Miss Elliott, not because he loved her, but influenced wholly by other and base considerations.

An old adage says, "the better anything is in its ligitimate sphere, the worse it is when otherwise employed." Lewis no doubt would have been an honorable and useful man, if he had married Naomi; he would then have been using the highest and strongest principle of human nature in a proper manner. In an evil hour he listened to the tempter, he turned aside from the ways of honor and truth. His eyes became blinded, conscience, the star of human destiny, lost her polarity, and the fierce storms drove his proud ship into the maelstrom of ruin. Jonathan Lewis was no more the proud, manly gentleman; he was henceforth a hard hearted, merciless wretch. He was a hyena skulking about the pathway of life, ready alike to kill the living, and to tear the dead from their graves. He not only resolved to forsake a lovely damsel, but first to ruin her fair name. His resolve was accomplished. He might have foreseen that this would ruin his prospects with the beautiful Miss Elliott; but the "wicked are blind and fall into the pit their own hands have digged." There are many young men now moving in high society, that think violets were created to be crushed by haughty boot heels; that desert flowers should rather be blasted than waste their sweetness on the air; that pearls should rather adorn a Cyclops, than sparkle in their native deep. Not so, ye canibals. If names must be blasted and characters ruined, in the name of heaven, let your victims come from among the affluent and the honorable. Who will pity and protect the poor daughter of shame; who will give her a crumb of bread? The more wealthy victim might, at least have bread to eat, water to drink and wherewithall to be clothed. Ye fair, blooming daughters of poverty, shun the advances of those who avoid you in company, as you would shun the grim monster death.

Lewis, aware that a period was approaching that would

mar all his hopes, unless they should immediately be consummated, urged his suit with all possible haste. Miss Elliott, however, baffled him on every tack, and, though she encouraged him, gave him but little hope of succeeding immediately. In the meanwhile, Naomi urged the fulfilment of his promise, that he would marry her forthwith, seconded by the power of tears and prayers. When these means seemed unavailing, she threatened him with the law. Lewis alarmed at this, charged her, at peril of life, to remain silent; he told her that their marriage was sure, but that very peculiar circumstances required all to be kept silent. But before he could bring matters to an issue with Miss Elliott, rumor whispered abroad the engagement and disgrace of Naomi Wise. This rumor fell like thunder upon Lewis; the depths of a dark but powerful soul were awakened, his hopes were quivering upon a balance which the next breath threatened with ruin. With a coolness and steadiness which innocence is wont to wear, Lewis affirmed to Miss Elliott that said rumor was a base, malicious slander, circulated by the enemies of the Lewis family, to ruin his character, and offered that time, a very fair arbiter, should decide upon the report, and if adjudged guilty, he would relinquish all claim to her, Miss Elliott's hand. For several days Lewis was apparently uneasy, appeared abstracted, neglected his business, and was not a little ill. Mr. Elliott assigned one cause, Miss Elliott another, but the true one was unknown to any one. The kingdom was in commotion, dark deeds were in contemplation, and at length the die was cast. Mrs. Adams had frequently of late told Naomi, that Lewis did not intend to marry her, that he was playing a game of villiany, and that she should place no further confidence in any of his assertions; but the poor girl thought or hoped differently; she could not and would not believe that Jonathan Lewis was untrue. Woman's love cannot doubt. Lewis at length came to see Miss Wise, and told her that he wished not to delay the marriage any longer; that he had made all necessary arrangements, and that he would come and take her to the house of a magistrate on a certain day. She urged the propriety of the marriage taking place at the house of Mr. Adams; but he refused and she without much reluctance consented to his wishes. Time sped on, the last morn rolled up the eastern vault in his chariot, dispensing light and joy to millions; Naomi walked forth with light heart and step, thinking only of her coming nuptials. During the day in the midst of her anticipations, gloomy forebodings would disturb her. Like the light breeze preceding the storm, they seemed to come and go without cause. So true is it;

"'That coming events cast their shadows before." She told nothing of what was about to take place to Mr. Adams; but at the appointed time taking the water pail in her hand, she went to the spring, the place at which she had agreed to meet Lewis. He soon appeared and took her behind him. It is said, that the stump off which Naomi mounted, remains to this day, and may be seen by any one who will visit New Salem,

> The last lone relic of Naomi's love,
> A speaking monument of a wretch's heart;
> Like love, its grasp time scarce can move,
> Like treachery, corruption lurks in every part.

The strong steed bore Naomi rapidly from the home of her childhood and youth; from the kind Mrs. Adams that was wont to soothe in every trouble.

CHAPTER III.

Naomi very soon perceived that they were not approaching the magistrate, by whose mystic knot sorrow was to be killed and joy born; but to her great surprise, Lewis kept the direct road to the river, speaking to her in the mean time with rather a strange voice and an incoherant manner. She tried to imagine his object, but she was convinced that he would not take her to Asheboro, and she knew of no magistrate in that direction; every effort therefore failed to give her troubled mind any peace. Slackening his pace to a slow walk, Lewis and Naomi held the following conversation.

"Naomi, which do you think is easiest, a slow or sudden death?"

"I'm sure I don't know, but what makes you ask me that question?"

"Why, I was just thinking about it. But which would you prefer, if you could have choice?"

"I would try to be resigned to whatever Providence

might appoint, and since we cannot have a choice, it is useless to have any preferences."

"Well, Naomi, do you think you would like to know the time when you are to die?"

"Why, Jonathan, what do you mean by such questions? I have never thought of such matters; and I am sure, I never knew you to be mentioning such things before."

Lewis rode on for some time without making any reply; seeming in a deep revery; but in fact in the most intense excitement; at length he remarked:

"Well, Naomi, I believe I know both the time and manner of your death, and I think it is in my power to give you a choice."

This ran through the poor girl like a dart of death; it was some minutes before she could make any reply.

"For the Lord's sake, Jonathan, what do you mean; do you intend to kill me, or why do you talk so?"

"I will never harm you; we shall be married in two hours. As you see, I am not going to——as I first intended, but am going across the river, where we shall have a nice wedding."

"Jonathan, I'm afraid every thing is not right, and I feel so bad this evening, I had rather go home and put it off till another day."

"No, no, that will not do. I tell you again, you need not fear any thing. Just be perfectly contented, and fear no harm from him that loves you better than himself."

They were now on a high bluff that commanded an extensive view of the river and the country beyond. The bold, rocky channel of the stream was distinctly visible for a great distance to the southeast; whilst from the northwest came the river, now swollen by recent rains, roaring and tumbling over rocky ledges, and then moving calmly away. A blue crane was flying slowly above the bed of the stream, whilst amid the dwarf pines and cedars that grew upon the crags, many ravens were cawing and screaming. This scenery, heightened by the dusk of evening, strongly impressed Naomi's mind. She remarked to Lewis:

"I am almost afraid to be in this lonely place; I wish we were away. O! how happy I should be, if we had a quiet home like yon from which that smoke is rising away over the hills. It may be foolishness, Jonathan, but I want you to be careful in going down these banks and crossing the river. I have so often feared something would happen to prevent the happiness we expect; and I am sure I never felt so bad in my life."

Lewis reined up his horse, stopped for a short time, then started forward, muttering, "I will though; I am a coward." Miss Wise asked him what he was saying; he replied that he only meant that they should be married that night. The river was here tolerably wide and below the ford some little turf-islands covered with alders and willows, made several sluices. Lewis rushed his horse in the water, which came up to his sides, and plunged forward rapidly till he reached the middle of the channel, then stopping his beast and turning himself in the saddle, he said to Naomi in a husky voice: "Naomi, I will tell you what I intend to do; I intend to drown you in this river; we can never marry. I found I could never get away from you, and I am determined to drown you."

"O! Jonathan, Jonathan," screamed the victim, "you do not, cannot mean what you say; do not terrify me so much and make haste out of here."

"I mean," said Lewis, just what I say; you will never go from here alive. You cannot move me by words or tears; my mind is fixed; I swear by all that's good or bad, that you have not five minutes to live. You have enticed me to injure my character, you have made me neglect my business. You ought never to have been such a fool as to expect that I would marry such a girl as you are. You did not expect that I was taking you off to marry you, when you got up behind me; you no doubt thought I would take you to Asheboro, and keep you there as a base ─────. Prepare to die."

"My Lord, what shall I do?" said Naomi, "You know I have loved you with my whole soul; I have trusted you, and when you betrayed me, I never reviled you. How often did I tell you that you did not intend to marry me! how many times did I beseech you to be honest with me! And after all, you certainly will not drown me. O, Jonathan, for heaven's sake take me out of this river! Do, O, do. O, spare my life! I will never ask you to marry me, I will leave the country, I will never mention your name again, and"───

Lewis stopped short her entreaties by grasping her throat with his left hand; her struggles immediately threw them both from the horse. Being a tall, strong man, he held her above the water until he tied her dress above her head, and then held her under beneath his foot until he was alarmed by a glare of torches approaching along the road he had just come. He mounted his horse and dashed out of the river on the south side.

Mrs Davis lived at no great distance from the river, and had heard the death screaming of poor Naomi. She had heard the startling cry as the villian caught her by the throat; then she heard the wild wail when she arose from the water, and lastly the stifled sobs as she was muffled in her dress. The old lady called her boys and bid them hasten to the ford, that somebody was murdered or drowned; but they were afraid to go, they hesitated and parlied; at last they set out with glaring torches, but it was too late. They arrived only in time to hear the murderer leaving the opposite bank. They neither saw nor heard Naomi. She was already dead, her last scream had died away, her last gasping groan had arisen through the rippling waters, and her body was floating amid the willows of a turf-island. A pure and beautiful damsel, she attracted the admiration of a cold-hearted world without gaining its respect; her pathway had been waylaid by those who thought poor, unprotected beauty bloomed only to be blasted. Her pure and ardent affections having never enjoyed the sunshine of love were ready to grasp the first support that offered. She had given her heart to a deceiver; she had trusted her life to a destroyer, and the murmuring waves that now bathed her lifeless form, and rocked her on their cold bosom, were the only agents perhaps, that had ever acted towards her without selfishness.

Early on the next morning the people of her home were searching in all directions for Naomi Mrs. Adams had passed a sleepless night; a strange impression had instantly fixed itself upon her mind as soon as Naomi was missed; and in her broken slumbers during the night, she was aroused by sometimes imagining that Naomi called her, at other times by dreaming that she saw her dead, and again by thinking she heard her screaming. At early dawn she aroused the vicinity, and going to the spring, the tracks of a horse were readily discovered and by the sign it was evident that Naomi had mounted from the stump. The company followed the track until Mrs Davis and her boys were met coming in haste to tell the circumstances of the preceding evening. The old lady told the crowd of the screaming she had heard; that the boys had gone down with the lights and heard a horseman galloping from the opposite bank.

"Ah!" said the old lady, "murder's been done, sich unyearthly screams can't come of nothing; they made the hair rise on my head, and the very blood curdle in my heart. No doubt poor Naomi's been drowned. O! ef I had been young as I once was, I would a run down there and killed the rascal afore he could a got away! What is the world a coming to?"

The company hastened to the river, and in a few moments discovered the body still muffled in the clothing. She was quickly borne to the shore and laid upon a rock; upon the fair neck of the dead were still to be seen the marks of the ruffian's fingers. The Coroner was sent for, the jury summoned, and the verdict pronounced, "Drowned by violence." Some one of the vast crowd now assembled, suggested that Lewis should be sought and brought to the corpse ere it was interred. This was assented to by acclamation, but who would do it? Who would dare to apprehend a Lewis? A firm, brave officer of Randolph accepted the task, and having selected his company from the numerous candidates, for every youth on the ground offered, proceeded to Asheboro."

So soon as Lewis saw the lights coming while he was at his work of death, as above said, he dashed out of the river, having no doubt that the water would bear the body into the deep pools below the ford, and render discovery impossible. We have seen that in this he was disappointed. Leaving the river, he rode rapidly around to another ford, and hastened to his father's near Centre meeting house. He dashed into the room where his mother was sitting, and asked for a change of clothes. The old lady alarmed, asked him why he came at that time of week (for he usually came on Sunday), why he was wet, and why he looked so pale and spoke in such a strange voice. He replied that he had started home on some business, and that his horse had fallen with him in the river, and that his wet clothes made him look pale and altered in his voice. His mother had too much sagacity to believe such a tale, but she could obtain from him no other explanation. Having procured a change of apparel, he departed and arrived at Asheboro early next morning. Riding up to Col. Craven's he called at the door: Mrs. Craven answered the call, and exclaimed in astonishment:

"What's the matter, Lewis, what have you been doing, have you killed 'Omi Wise?

Lewis was stunned; raising his hand and rubbing his eyes, he said:

"Why what makes you ask me that question?"

"No particular reason," said Mrs. Craven, "only you look so pale and wild; you don't look at all like yourself this morning."

Lewis made no reply, but the flushed countenance which he exhibited, would have afforded no small evidence to a close observer, that something was wrong. So true is it, "That the wicked flee when no man pursueth." Leaving Asheboro, Lewis went to a sale at a Mr. Hancock's at a place now owned by Thomas Cox. During the day it was remarked by many that Jonathan Lewis had a cast countenance by no means usual. Instead of that bold, daring independence that was usual to him, he seemed reserved, downcast and restless. By indulging freely in drink, which was always to be had on such occasions he became more like himself toward evening; and even ventured to mingle with the ladies. For it should be observed, that in those days, the ladies attended vendues, elections, musters, &c., without derogation to their characters. And in very many places, a young man showed his gallantry by collecting the fair ones whom he would honor and conducting them to some wagon, where his liberality was displayed by purchasing cakes, cider, &c. Let it not be supposed that this custom was confined to the low or vulgar, for the practice was well nigh universal. Our lady readers must not think it beneath their dignity to read of such characters, for our mothers, and perhaps their's also, have received such treats. Lewis on the occasion above named, seemed particular attracted by Martha, the daughter of Stephen Huzza. After waiting upon her according to the manner of the times Lewis accompanied her home. The manner of courting at that day, was very different from what now prevails; the custom then was, for the young people to remain in the room after the old people retired, then seat themselves beside each other, and there remain until 12 or 1 o'clock. Lewis had taken his seat and drawn Martha into his lap; rather a rude move even at that time, and not a little contrary to Martha's will—when a gentle rap was heard at the door. While the inmates were listening to hear it repeated, the door opened, and Robert Murdock, the brave officer who had pursued Lewis, entered, attended by a retinue that at once overawed the unarmed murderer. He suffered himself to be quietly arrested and taken back to the river bank where his victim still remained. He put his hand upon her face, and smoothed her hair, apparently unmoved. So greatly was the crowd incensed at this hard hearted audacity, that the authority of the officer was scarcely sufficient to prevent the villian's being killed upon the spot. The evidence against Lewis, though circumstantial, was deemed conclusive. The foot-prints from the stump to the river exactly fitted his horse; hairs upon the skirt on which she rode, were found to fit in color; a small piece torn from Lewis' accoutrement, fitted both rent and texture; his absence from Asheboro,' and many other minuter circumstances all conspired to the same point. In proper form he was committed to jail in Asheboro,' to await his trial. A vast company on the next day attended the remains of Naomi to the grave. The whole community mourned her untimely death; the aged wiped the falling tear from their wrinkled faces; the young men stood there in deep solemnity, and sighed over the fair one now pale in death; many very many maidens wept over betrayed and blasted innocence, and all were melted in grief, when the shroud hid the face of Naomi forever.

The writer knows not the place of her grave else would he visit that lonely place! he would place at her head a simple stone, to tell her name, her excellence and her ruin; he would plant there appropriate emblems, and drop a tear over the memory of her who sleeps beneath.

> "Oh! fair as the wild flower, close to thee growing,
> How pure was thy heart till love's witchery came,
> Like the wind of the South oe'r a summer lute blowing
> It hushed all its music and withered its fame,
> The young village maid, when with flowers she dresses
> Her dark flowing hair for some festival day,
> Will think of thy fate till neglecting her tresses
> She mournfully turns from the mirror away."

CHAPTER IV.

Though Lewis was confined in the strong jail, that then towered in Asheboro' as a terror to evil doers, his was not the character to yield without an effort; and such was his strength, skill or assistance, that he soon escaped. He broke jail and fled to parts unknown. Time rolled on, bearing upon its ever changing surface new scenes, actions and subjects of thought. Naomi was beginning to fade from memory, and Lewis was scarcely thought of. The whole tragedy would, perhaps, have been nearly in the sea of oblivion, but for the song of "*Omi Wise*," which was sung in every neighborhood. At length, rumor, the persecutor and avenger, gave tidings that Jonathan Lewis was living at the falls of Ohio, was married, had one child, and considered in prosperous circumstances. The murdered girl rose fresh in the minds of the people. Justice cried, "cut the sinner down." Indignation cried shame to the lingering servants of law. Col. Craven, Col. Lane and George Swearengain, properly commissioned, started in quest of the criminal. Many were the sighs and expressions of anxieties that escaped their friends, when these worthy citizens departed. All were aware that the enterprise was perilous. Most of the Lewis family had migrated to the same region, and one Lewis was not trifled with, much less a community of such personages. But brave men, especially of Randolph county, sustained by justice, never count the foe, or ask a parley. Having arrived in the neighborhood, or rather in the country, for they were yet many miles from Lewis' home, they made inquiry until they found the circumstances and position of the families. Knowing, that if they appeared in person, their object would be defeated, they hired two sturdy hunters for a fee of seventy five dollars, to take Jonathan, dead or alive, and deliver him at a certain town. "No work, no pay." The three officers went to the town to await the issue, and it it failed, to collect if possible, such force as might be necessary to wage civil war upon the whole offending tribe.

The hunters, unknown to the Lewises, having arrived in the immediate vincinity, learned that a great dance was to take place that night at a house in the neighborhood, and that all the Lewises would be there. They concluded that the occasion would either enable them to execute their object, or at least to make some useful observations; they accordingly rode to the place, in appearance and profession two wandering backwoodsmen. Arriving at the rude fence in front of the house, and seeing a considerable number already collected, one of the hunters cried:

"Hallo to the man of the house and all his friends."

"Hallo back to you." said a voice within, "and maybe you'd light and look at your saddle."

"Apt as not," said the hunter, "if wer'e allowed to see our saddles on the peg, our horses eatin' fodder, and ourselves merry over hog and hominy."

"Ef you are what you look like," said the landlord, stepping into the yard, "and not Yankee speculators, nor bamboozled officers, nor Natchez sharpers, you are welcome to sich as we have."

"And spose we are not what we look like," replied the hunter "what then?"

"Why' the sooner you move your washing, the better; wer'e plain honest folks here, and deal with all scatterlopers arter their deserts."

"Well, well, we'll light and take some of your pone and a little of your blinkeye, and maybe as how we'll get better acquainted."

So saying, the strangers alighted, and having seen their horses supplied with a bountiful quantity of provender, they entered the house and mingled with the guests without exciting suspicion or even much notice. They had previously agreed, that one should do the talking, lest they might commit some incongruities. A glance convinced them that Jonathan Lewis was not there. The guests continued to assemble, women, men and children; an old wrinkled-faced vagabond commenced tuning his violin and the parties were arranging themselves for the dance, when a strong powerful man entered. His hair was long, bushy and matted as if it had never known the virtue of a comb: his eyebrows were dark and heavy; his step was decided and firm: he wore a belted hunting shirt in the band of which hung a long, double-edged hunting knife, and under its folds were plainly visible two heavy pistols. His keen eye detected the strangers instantly, and forthwith he sought the landlord at the other end of the house, and engaged him for a time in whispers. Our hunters knew their man, and watched him with no small anxiety, nor was it long until he approached them and said:

"I reckon you're strangers in these parts."

"I reckon we are too, being we know nobody and nobody knows us; and we're perlight enough not to trouble strangers with foolish questions, and so I guess we shall still be strangers."

This answer to his implied question evidently displeased the interrogator; after eyeing them a moment, he continued,

"But maybe we all come from the same land, and so might scrape an acquaintance easier than you think,"

"As to that, it's no difference, without telling or asking names, we give the right hand to every honest hunter."

"Then you're hunters, I spose, and as we have a great deer hunt tomorrow, perhaps you'll join."

"That we will, ef its agreeable."

The dance passed off without anything remarkable, and early next morning the horns were sounding, the dogs yelping and everything alive for the hunt. In arranging the couples to stand at the crosses, it so happened that Jonathan and our talking hunter were stationed together, and the other stranger at no great distance. The drivers had departed, and the marksmen were reclining at ease or examining their firelocks, when Jonathan discovered that he had no powder. As it would probably be an hour or two before the game would appear, Lewis proposed to his companion that they should go to the village and supply themselves with powder. They had no sooner started, than the other hunter discovered his comrade to give the signal, he accordingly followed at some distance in the rear. Close by the village he met Lewis and his companion on their return. The hunters exchanged signs and agreed to make the effort; they were fully aware of their peril; for though two against one, they knew their antagonist to be much more powerful than either, and to be well armed. The hunter that met them, pretended that he had become alarmed when he missed them, not knowing what might happen, and that he had come in search; then asking about the powder, requested to see some. While Lewis was pouring some into his hand, the other seized him from behind in order to hold his hands fast; while the front man grasping him by the legs, endeavored to throw him. Like a second Sampson, Lewis tore his arms from the grasp of the hunter, and with a back-handed blow sent him near a rod backwards, at the same time kicking down the man that was before him. But before he could level his gun the first hunter gave him such a blow with the barrel of his gun that he reeled and fell; but pointing his gun as the second hunter came, he would have shot him dead, if the other had not struck his arm; the flash of the gun, however, set fire to the powder, that in the melee, had been spilled upon the hunter's clothes and scorched the whole company not a little. Lewis better capable of enduring such catastrophes than the others, taking advantage of the confusion, would have made his escape, had not the villagers arrived in sufficient strength to overpower him by force of numbers.

Col. Craven and his companions received Lewis bound with strong cords and immediately started for Carolina, nor did they travel at a moderate rate, well knowing that if the Lewis family with their confederates should overtake them, death would be the fate of the weaker party; nor did the hunters tarry in the vicinity but hurried themselves far away in the western wilds. After Lewis found that further resistance would be useless he seemed to submit to his fate and became tractable and social, so much so, that his bonds were somewhat slackened and his captivity less strict. He awakened no suspicion by asking them to be less cautious, and seemed so much more social than they had ever known him, that his guards were almost tempted to free him from all restraint. One evening while indulging their glee around the camp fire, Lewis unobserved untied his bonds, and springing up, darted off with the agility of a youth Craven and Swearengain pursued, but Craven was ere long left some distance in the rear. They were now in a low bottom and the evening had so far advanced that Swearengain, who was close in pursuit, could only see Lewis by the whiteness of his clothes. So expert was Lewis in dodging that he constantly eluded the grasp of his pursuer and was now within a few paces of a dense thicket, Swearengain making a spring, struck Lewis with a blow so effectual that it felled him to the earth, and before he could regain his feet, he was overpowered by both of his pursuers.

Lewis was finally brought to Randolph from which county his trial was moved to Guilford, where he was finally tried and acquitted. Most of the material witnesses had died or moved away and much of the minutæ, was forgotten. After his release he returned to Kentucky and died in a few years afterwards. After all hopes of his recovery was given up, and his friends watched around his couch only to perform the last sad offices of life, he still lingered. He seemed to suffer beyond human conception; the contortions of his face were too horrid for human gaze; his groans were appalling to the ear. For two days the death rattle had been in his throat, and yet he retained his reason and speech. Finally he bid every person leave the room but his father, and to him he confessed all the circumstances we have detailed. He declared that while in prison, Naomi was ever before him; his sleep was broken by her cries for mercy, and in the dim twilight her shadowy form was ever before him, holding up her imploring hands. Thus ended the career of Jonathan Lewis, for no sooner was his confession completed than his soul seemed to hasten away.

The following is the song so well known in this county, as

POOR NAOMI.

Come all you good people, I'd have you draw near,
A sorrowful story you quickly shall hear;
A story I'll tell you about N'omi Wise,
How she was deluded by Lewis' lies.

He promised to marry and use me quite well;
But conduct contrary I sadly must tell,
He promised to meet me at Adams' Springs,
He promised me marriage and many fine things.

Still nothing he gave but yet flattered the case,
He says, we'll be married and have no disgrace,
Come get up behind me, we'll go up to town,
And there we'll be married, in union be bound.

I got up behind him and straightway did go
To the banks of Deep river, where the water did flow:
He says, "Now, Naomi, I'll tell you my mind,
I intend here to drown you, and leave you behind."

O! pity your infant and spare me my life;
Let me go rejected and not be your wife.
"No pity, no pity," this monster did cry,
"In Deep river's bottom your body shall lie."

The wretch then did choke her, as we understand,
And threw her in the river, below the milldam.
Be it murder or treason, Oh! what a great crime
To murder poor Naomi and leave her behind.

Naomi was missing, they all did well know,
And hunting for her to the river did go;
And there found her floating on the water so deep,
Which caused all the people to sigh and to weep.

The neighbors were sent for to see the great sight,
While she lay floating all that long night,
So early next morning the inquest was held,
The jury correctly the murder did tell.

NOTE.—It is said that in the dusk of evening, the following little song may be heard about the river in accents sweet as angels sing:

> Beneath these crystal waters,
>   A maiden once did lie,
> The fairest of earth's daughters,
>   A gem to deck the sky.
>
> In caves of pearled enamel,
>   We weave a maiden's shroud
> For all the foolish damsels,
>   That dare to stray abroad.
>
> We live in rolling billows,
>   We float upon the mist,
> We sing on foaming pillows;
>   "Poor Naomi of the past."

On July 7th, 1879, Mr. J. B. Randleman and the present Naomi Falls Company commenced building a cotton factory, which to day stands as a monument of their energy and enterprise. There is now a beautiful town of about 500 inhabitants, and the hum of 5000 spindles and the clash of 164 looms and the voices of 225 employees is heard within less than 200 yards of the ford where the tragedy referred to in this book was enacted. This place was named in honor of Naomi, who was buried on the plantation upon which Calvin Swim now lives, in sight of Naomi Falls Factory. The spring where Naomi met Lewis and mounted his horse on the fatal night, is now used to supply water for the New Salem Steam Mill and Tannery Company. Mr. J. N. Caudle's barn now stands about where Mr. Adams' house then stood.

MANUFACTURING.

THE GREAT COTTON MILLS OF RANDOLPH COUNTY.

A Statistical Record and Descriptive Sketch of the Mills and their Surroundings.

THE NAOMI COTTON MILLS,
Randleman, N. C.

These great mills, the industrial monument to the memory of the beautiful but unfortunate Naomi Wise, were established a few years ago by the Naomi Falls Manufacturing Co., of which Mr. R. P. Dicks is treasurer and principal owner of the stock represented, which is about $180,000. Miss Mamie Pomeroy, than whom there is perhaps no more accurate acountant in this sunny land of flowers and fair women, has charge of the company's books.

Mr. Dicks, assisted by his fair book-keeper has the general supervision of every detail pertaining to the management of this gigantic enterprise. He is a shrewd business man, generous and kind hearted and is thoroughly posted in the manufacture of goods in his line.

Rev. A. Gregson, general superintendent has charge of all the departments managed by the following subordinates;

Mr. F. C. Furgerson, manager spinning department; Mr. J. A. Wright, manager weaving department; Mr. Marsh Hughes, chief engineer, assisted by Mr Dave Laughlin.

These gentlemen have charge of 260 employees, to whom the treasurer pays annually about $50,000. There are 5,000 spindles and 226 looms, all of which are placed in one grand brick structure 52x105 feet in dimensions, one story and a basement the same length and width. This great building has a metal roof, in the centre of which, and just above the main entrance, there is a cupola bearing a large tank filled with water to be used in case of fire. The mills work about 2,500 bales of cotton per year from which the 5,000 spindles, kept constantly at work, produce the immense quantity of 1,000,000 pounds of warp of different numbers, annually. A large portion of this is used in the manufacture of about 400 styles of beautiful plaids, &c., and the remainder is converted into excellent grain bags. The value of plaids manufactured is about $200,000, and that of bags $50,000, making the grand total of $250,000 annual business.

The dimensions of the principal buildings connected with the main building are as follows: Managed by J. H. Wilson. Dye house 35x85, Managed by J. E. McLaughen. Baling house 40x50, lapper house 35x50, boiler house 35x40, engine house 20x30 feet.

The office, one of the finest and best arranged in the State, is a handsome brick building 30x48 feet in dimensions, with three compartments for the treasurer, book keeper and superintendent respectively.

There are about 75 dwellings occupied by the employees and officers of the company, the most beautiful of which is the mansion occupied by the treasurer. This building cost $10,000.

The motive power of the mammoth cotton mill described in the foregoing sketch, consists of one 150 H. P. Harris Corless engine and two 48 in, Leffell water wheels. The boiler plant consists of three 60 H. P. return tubular boilers and is located under the same roof with the engine.

In connection with the manufacturing business the company owns a large store which is managed by Mr. W. J. Glass, assisted by Messrs Steed and Lamb as salesmen. These gentlemen carry an elegant line of general merchandise and sell $50,000 worth of goods annually. The brick building occupied is 30x115 in dimensions, two story and basement, and is located near the factory.

Just above this great cotton mill and in the town of Randleman, there is another mammoth mill, located on Deep River, which is the pioneer of all other cotton mills in Randolph county.

THE RANDLEMAN COTTON MILLS

RANDLEMAN MANUFACTURING CO., PROP's.

These mammoth mills are located about 3 1-2 miles

from Millboro, the present terminus of the branch road intersecting with the C. F. & Y. V. Railroad at Factory Junction, Mr. John H. Ferree is the principal owner of the stock representing about $200,000, and is Treasurer of the Company which is composed of the following persons. Messrs. J. H. Ferree, L. H. Weaver and Charley C. Randleman, Mr. S. G. Newlin, assisted by Mr. J. T. Millican, has charge of the books and is assistant Treasurer. Mr. J. O. Pickard is the general superintendent and has served in that capacity for a number of years.

Mr. Charley Randleman is the chief manager of the spinning department. This young man is a son of the late John Randleman who was at his death one of the principal owners of the mill bearing his name.

Mr. W. T. Furguson, in charge of the beaming department, has been connected with the mill for about 12 years and will have served the company 14 years on the termination of his present contract.

Mr. M. L. Ellington, assisted by Mr. William Ivey, controls the employees of the weaving department. Mr. John Clapp, for 12 years in the company's employ, has charge of the two large dying establishments. The baling department is in charge of Mr. J. E. Hayworth, a gentleman of experience and for a long time connected with the mills. Mr. J. A. Myricks is chief engineer and assistant superintendent, assisted by Mr. H. H. Nelson.

Mr. Myricks is a very fine engineer as will be proven by the engine recently set up by him which is so nicely adjusted that a nickle coin placed edgewise on the cylinder head will not jar off when the engine is in motion.

The number of employees connected with these great cotton mills is 245 to whom the company pays the handsome sum of $44,824 per annum.

The mills consume about 1,900 bales, or nearly 2,000,000 pounds of cotton, annually. From this immense quantity they produce about 800,000 lbs warp, running 4,272 spindles, 222 looms are employed in the manufacture of about 3,536,000 yards of over 700 different styles of beautiful plaids, the value of which is about $247,520.

The machinery named above is placed in two large buildings, one of which is a brick building, two stories high, 40x100 feet in dimension, with a wing 40x80 feet one story. The other is a wooden building 36x300 feet in dimensions, one story.

The two dye houses are 22x82 feet each, lapper house 40x50, baling house 35x70, warping house 30x30, two stories, engine and boiler houses, each, 20x30, and a large three story brick building, 30x70 feet, used as a town hall. On the first floor of this building, and in the rear, is the principal office of the company.

The motive power of this mill consists one 100 H. P. Harris-Corles engine, and two 44 in. and one 40 in. Leffell water wheels, working under 13 feet head of water.

The boiler plant consists of two 75 H P., and one 60 H. P. return tubular boilers, manufactured by Talbott & Sons, Richmond, Va.

There are about 150 dwellings including the handsome residences occupied by the proprietors and officers. The value of the whole property is about $200,000.

There are about 300 dwellings in the town of Randleman proper, including 5 churches, 3 school houses, 2 hotels, 10 or more stores and shops 1 tin shop, 3 blacksmith shops and other smaller enterprises. The population is about 2,000. The principal store is owned by the Randleman Store Co. The building is 3 stories high with basement and is about 40x130 feet in dimensions. The salesmen are Messrs. N. N. and J. J. Newlin, and H. D. Scarboro. The annual sales amount to something near $50,000, which, including the annual sales of the Naomi store, the Naomi cotton mills and Randleman cotton mills amounts to the immense sum of $597,520 per annum. Both the above mills use Electric lights.

www.ingramcontent.com/pod-product-compliance
Lightning Source LLC
Chambersburg PA
CBHW022140160426
43197CB00009B/1371